The Consumer Guide to Over-the-Counter Drugs

Robert P. Mauch, Jr., Pharm. D., Ph.D.
Susan A. Mauch, R.Ph.

The information about drugs contained in this book is general in nature and is intended for use as an educational aid. It does not cover all possible uses, actions, precautions, side effects, or interactions of these medicines, nor is the information intended as medical advice for individual problems or for making an evaluation as to the risks and benefits of taking a particular drug. You should consult your doctor or pharmacist before taking any particular drug.

© Copyright 1997 Prescriptive Analysis, Inc.

Published in the U.S.A. by
Strategies for Growth, Inc.
ISBN 0–9657918–0–7
All rights reserved. No part of this book may be reproduced in any form or by any means without written permission from the publisher.

Library of Congress Catalog Card No.: 97–066239

Mauch, Robert P., Jr., Pharm D., Ph.D.
Mauch, Susan A., R.Ph.
    1. Evaluating and understanding over-the-counter drug options
    2. Determining a self-treatment plan
    3. Comparing similar non-prescription medications side-by-side

This book was designed and produced by
Strategies for Growth, Inc.
Medina, Ohio

Cover Design: Ross Brandt Graphics

Table of Contents

Index of Tables

Acknowledgments

Eckerd Corporation wishes to express its gratitude to our Editorial Review Board for their assistance and participation in the development of this book.

Susan A. Mauch, R.Ph.
Senior Editor, Review Board Coordinator
Prescriptive Analysis, Inc.
Palm Harbor, Florida

George Dickens, Pharm.D.
University of Kentucky
Medical College
Lexington, Kentucky

Paul Doering, M.S.P.
University of Florida
College of Pharmacy
Gainesville, Florida

James C. Eoff, Pharm.D.
University of Tennessee
College of Pharmacy
Memphis, Tennessee

Richard Fiscella, M.P.H.
University of Illinois at
Chicago College of
Pharmacy
Chicago, Illinois

William Hopkins, Pharm.D.
Mercer University Southern
School of Pharmacy
Atlanta, Georgia

Victor Padron, Ph.D.
Creighton University School
of Pharmacy and Allied
Health Professions
Omaha, Nebraska

Farid Sadik, Ph.D.
University of South
Carolina College of
Pharmacy
Columbia, South Carolina

Kay Sadik, R.Ph.
University of South
Carolina College of
Pharmacy
Columbia, South Carolina

Ralph Small, Pharm.D.
Virginia Commonwealth
University School of
Pharmacy
Richmond, Virginia

Dennis Thompson, Pharm.D.
Southwestern Oklahoma
State University
Oklahoma City, Oklahoma

Introduction

Throughout history, people have sought solutions and answers to medical problems through **self-medication**—that is, through treating themselves.

Today, as well, Americans are often quick to treat their ailments without professional help. This self-treatment involves over-the-counter (OTC) medications about 60 percent of the time

The OTC industry continues to blossom and grow. As Americans, we spend tens of billions of dollars every year on self-medicating products. Yet with all the billions of dollars being spent, self-medication with OTC medications is one of the *least costly* components of our entire health-care system.

This relationship between the low cost of OTC medications and the entire health-care system becomes even more dramatic when you consider the cost of self-treatment in these terms: Sixty percent of the medications purchased in the United States are OTC products, yet OTC medication expenditures represent **less than two cents** of the entire health-care dollar.

The role of OTC medications is changing, too. In the past, OTC medications were once intended only to relieve symptoms. Today, many products that were available only by prescription are now available as over-the-counter products. Not only do they relieve symptoms, they can actually be used as a treatment or cure for an illness.

The key to successfully treating any disease or illness is to **choose the proper product.** This task is not always easy. To do it right, self-treatment involves a decision-making process that includes recognition of symptoms, judgment of severity, and choice and assessment of treatment options.

The Eckerd Consumer Guide to Over-the-Counter Drugs has been carefully designed to help you identify specific symptoms of different diseases and conditions, and to guide you in choosing the appropriate over-the-counter (OTC) product or products to best treat your symptoms.

Each chapter briefly discusses a particular disease, its cause or causes, symptoms, severity, and the best way to treat it. For example, in Chapter 1, we talk about the common cold and allergic rhinitis. We define the symptoms of both and lead you through a series of steps to help you locate the perfect OTC medication for your particular symptoms.

This book has been written and designed by pharmacists to help you treat your illness as specifically as possible. Always remember that your Eckerd Pharmacist is available for questions and that his primary mission is to help you and your family stay healthy.

We hope you will find the information contained in this book helpful and, more important, easy to use. We welcome your comments.

Saving Money Without Sacrificing Quality

Many OTC products are now available in generic form. This allows you to have the same medication offered by the brand-name products, but often at a much lower price. Your Eckerd Pharmacy offers a vast variety of these lower-cost versions of the pricier brand-name OTC products. They are located on the shelf just beside the brand-name products. Although Eckerd Brand products may be packaged differently and may be called by another name, the active ingredient or ingredients are the same as the brand-name products. All Eckerd Brand products are fully guaranteed.

If price is a factor, take the time to look for these Eckerd Brand products. There are **no differences in quality**.

The First Line of Defense

Self-medication is often the first line of defense in treating an illness. Understanding your body and its signs and symptoms is the key to keeping your body healthy. When symptoms appear, they must be properly assessed and treated accordingly.

You can do this quite effectively when you take the time to identify the symptoms, recognize their severity, and if needed, choose the proper product.

Education is a must! Often people have been taught certain things concerning health that are **incorrect** or they have **misinterpreted** certain information. Educate yourself with the latest knowledge. If you feel uncertain about a symptom or disease, consult your Eckerd Pharmacist or physician.

Although OTC medications can be effectively used to treat the symptoms associated with illness or disease (or the disease or illness itself), if the wrong product is chosen for use, the consequences can prove harmful and at times, even fatal.

One study concluded that approximately one-third of those people who self-treated their symptoms had used ineffective treatments because they selected the wrong product or products.

The elder segment of our population often treat themselves ineffectively. Some studies report that as many as 65 percent of the elder population use at least one OTC product daily. Another study concluded that 55 percent of its elder sample were taking from one to nine self-prescribed drugs at any given time. This study also found that 33.1 percent of the group took unknown drugs, 66.6 percent took analgesics (15 percent misused aspirin), 30 percent took laxatives (2.7 percent misused), 29.3 percent took vitamins (6.3 percent misused), and 26.4 percent took antacids (6.3 percent misused).

As frequent users of OTC medications, the elderly are susceptible to the many detrimental side effects of over-the-counter medication use. The elderly have altered absorption, metabolism, distribution, and excretion of drug compounds. In addition to these problems, the elderly have a greater potential for sight and hearing impairment than found in younger people. And so, because of these potential impairments, the elderly have a greater likelihood of having a "misadventure" when using an OTC product.

In all groups—especially with the elderly—special precautions must be taken when choosing the appropriate OTC products.

Good Communication Is the Key

Good communication is necessary to ensure that you receive the best health care possible. This includes not only communicating with yourself and listening to your body, but communicating with your Eckerd Pharmacist, your physician, and your health care provider. Remember, their job is to help you!

If you see more than one physician, make sure that each physician you see knows what other medications you are taking. And make sure each has your complete history of illnesses or diseases. For example, if your eye doctor tells you that you have glaucoma and places you on a medication, make certain that you give this information to all of your other doctors and to your pharmacist as well.

Otherwise, one physician may place you on a medication that adversely reacts with one that you already take or is similar to one that you take.

Many emergency situations and unnecessary hospitalizations occur each year due to the fact that people take duplicate-type medications and have serious reactions.

It is a good idea to carry a card with you at all times listing any diseases, medications, allergies, etc., that you have, as well as telephone numbers of friends or relatives who can be reached in case of an emergency.

There may be a time or situation when you will be unable to communicate this information to a health care provider. This information could be vital.

Also, it is a very good idea to shop at and continue to return to the same Eckerd Pharmacy so that your personal medical history and list of all medications can be kept in one place and monitored. Our pharmacy computers allow our pharmacists to record all of your medications, food, drug or dye allergies, diagnoses, age, weight, and so on.

This enables the pharmacist to monitor your medications specifically for you. Make sure that your Eckerd Pharmacist has your **most current** medical history on file. This history should include any new diagnoses, allergies and medications (Rx or OTC) that you take.

Your Eckerd Pharmacist's primary mission is to help keep you healthy. If you have any medical concerns, please talk to him or her. Your Eckerd Pharmacist is here for you.

It's right at Eckerd!

A Century of Service

The *Century of Service* we currently enjoy at Eckerd Pharmacy is based on a tradition of quality and service that began 100 years ago. Today, each of our more than 8,000 pharmacists at 2,800 Eckerd Pharmacies in 24 states exemplifies that same dedication and commitment to quality and service.

You will find that each of our Eckerd Pharmacists listens carefully to your questions, and then provides you with the answers you need. Our pharmacists are constantly updating their skills, too, and utilizing state-of-the-art technology to its fullest.

We currently fill over <u>150 million prescriptions a year</u>—and we accept more than 3,000 insurance plans.

At Eckerd, we offer a low price guarantee. We won't be beat on prescription prices from AARP or any local competitor. If you find a lower price, we'll match it. <u>Guaranteed</u>.

Plus, when it comes to over-the-counter drugs, you learn quickly that Eckerd brand products save you (on average) 30 percent *every-day*. If you are not completely satisfied, return the unused portion for a full refund, or get the national-brand equivalent <u>free</u>.

Get updates to the information in this book at the **Eckerd Corporation Home Page** on the World Wide Web. Visit us at **www.eckerd.com.** We recommend you set this as a bookmark and visit often.

Chapter One

Choosing the Proper Cold or Allergic Rhinitis Product

The **common cold** affects millions of people every year. It is perhaps the single most expensive illness in the United States when you factor in the many physician visits, pharmacy visits, and lost work days that accompany it.

Like the common cold, **allergic rhinitis** (stuffy, runny nose) primarily affects the upper respiratory tract. While cold and rhinitis symptoms can be very similar, the causes are quite different, and you need to treat them differently.

Fortunately, over-the-counter (OTC) cold and allergy products and remedies are extremely effective in treating a wide range of symptoms associated with both the common cold and allergic rhinitis. However, with so many different OTC products to choose from—and each one with its own unique characteristics and claims—choosing the best product can prove both difficult and frustrating.

The key to selecting the right OTC cold or allergy product is to **identify** your symptoms *specifically* and then **treat** those symptoms as *specifically* as possible.

Physiology

Understanding the physiology of the respiratory system can help you correctly identify your symptoms.

As part of the upper respiratory tract, the nose is responsible for adding moisture to and warming the air you breathe, as well as for filtering or preventing foreign particles such as dust, bacteria, pollen or other pollutants from entering your body.

Instead of entering your body, these particles become trapped in the **mucosal lining** of the nose. This mucous is then passed from the nose into the **nasopharynx** where it is either swallowed or expectorated.

The **cough control center,** located in your brain, triggers a sequence of events that ultimately results in the **cough reflex.** The

11

purpose of the cough reflex is to protect your lungs by keeping them free of foreign particles by expelling air from your lungs.

Similarly, the **sneeze reflex** helps expel air through your nose and mouth, clearing the nasal passages of foreign particles.

Although the cough and sneeze reflexes act in your body's defense, they can prove quite bothersome and annoying. Appropriate OTC medications aid in effectively decreasing both the frequency and intensity of these reflexes, giving temporary relief from symptoms while the body's natural defense mechanisms go about the business of fighting off the illness.

Recognizing Your Symptoms: Cold Versus Flu

The common cold is caused by **viruses**. Cold symptoms occur quickly, progress rapidly, and disappear. Symptoms of a common cold generally last five (5) to seven (7) days.

When symptoms last for seven (7) to ten (10) days or more, you should consult a physician regarding what may be a more severe infection. The symptoms of the common cold often mimic the symptoms of **influenza** or the **flu.** Consequently, it is very helpful for you to be able to distinguish between the two. People who are most susceptible to the flu, or who have recurrent episodes, should consider the **flu vaccine** which is given annually.

CHART 1.1: Is It a Common Cold or Influenza?

Symptom	Common Cold	Influenza
Cough (usually dry)	Mild to moderate	Moderate to severe
Fever	Rare	Common
Fatigue	Mild	Severe
Headache	Rare	Common
Muscle and joint aches and pains	Slight	Common
Runny, stuffy nose	Common	Uncommon
Sneezing	Common	Uncommon
Sore throat	Common	Uncommon

Identifying a Bacterial Infection

Unlike a viral infection, a **bacterial infection,** when present, should be treated by your physician. It is often difficult to differentiate between viral and bacterial infections.

Symptoms of bacterial infections often occur rapidly and may include swollen lymph nodes, fever, sore throat, green-yellow discharge from the nasal area, and respiratory symptoms similar to those that accompany viral infections. If you suspect a bacterial infection, contact your physician immediately. Your physician will be able to diagnose your infection and treat it appropriately.

Identifying Allergic Rhinitis

Allergic rhinitis occurs as an allergic response to inhaled irritants. In other words, it is a sensitive reaction to one or more of a variety of "things" floating in the air.

Allergic rhinitis can be either **perennial** or **seasonal**. One of the most common forms of seasonal allergic rhinitis is **hay fever**.

As the names imply, the symptoms of perennial allergic rhinitis usually persist year round. Conversely, the symptoms of seasonal allergic rhinitis occur only at certain times of the year.

CHART 1.2: Causes of Perennial and Seasonal Allergic Rhinitis

Perennial Causes:

Environmental:
1. house dust mites
2. animal dander
3. feathers

Occupational:
1. wheat flour
2. various grains
3. cotton and flax seeds
4. detergents
5. paint fumes
6. topical sprays
7. industrial solvents

Non-specific:
1. tobacco smoke
2. chalk dust
3. road dust
4. heavily polluted air
5. drugs
6. foods

Seasonal Causes:

Environmental:
1. mold spores
2. tree pollen
3. ragweed pollen
4. grass pollen

Symptoms of allergic rhinitis—including sneezing, runny nose, nasal itching, and nasal congestion—can occur within seconds of exposure to irritants or allergens.

Some less common symptoms may include headache, earache, loss of smell and taste, and/or sore, dry, or watery eyes.

Sometimes, prolonged symptoms produce other serious symptoms. These may include a nagging or persistent cough, asthmatic wheezing, or a feeling of tightness in the chest. These additional symptoms may indicate **asthma.** You should consult a physician for proper diagnosis and treatment.

There are three primary methods for treating allergic rhinitis. First, you can **avoid the irritants** altogether. Depending on your allergy, avoidance may be relatively easy. For example, simply wearing a mask while mowing the lawn is an effective and viable strategy for avoiding both allergens and symptoms.

Second, you might find relief with **allergy shots.** You can ask a physician to establish a shot regimen that suits your specific needs. Your physician will design a shot regimen for you after a series of allergy tests are performed to determine your specific allergies.

Finally, many people turn to OTC **allergy medications** for relief. These medications are fast, effective, and easily accessible.

Allergic rhinitis is treated primarily with **antihistamines** and **decongestants,** and treated secondarily with **analgesics** and **antitussives.**

Choosing OTC Medications to Treat Colds or Allergic Rhinitis

There are so many OTC products to choose from that selecting the appropriate OTC medication can be both difficult and frustrating. Before you self-treat with an OTC medication, consider and follow these general guidelines.

If you have:

1. Increased secretions (i.e., runny nose, sneezing, watery eyes) . . . take an **antihistamine**

2. Congested nasal passages (i.e., stuffy nose) . . . take a **decongestant**

3. A productive cough (i.e., producing phlegm, or a congested chest) . . . take an **expectorant**

4. A dry, irritating cough
   . . . take an **anti-tussive**

5. Headache, body aches, sore throat, fever
   . . . take an **analgesic**

If you have the symptoms of the common cold, follow the diagram below to determine which type of product is best for you. For example, if you have a combination runny-stuffy nose and body aches, choose products containing an antihistamine, a decongestant, and an analgesic. Table 1-8 (page 30) identifies such products.

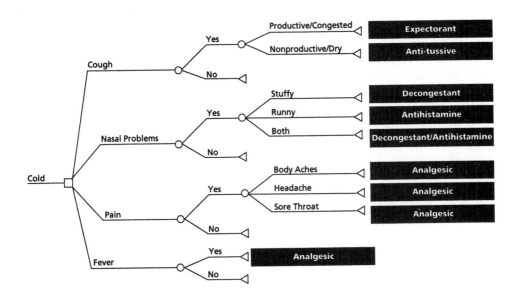

Antihistamines

Note: Antihistamines may also be used as sleep-inducing agents or to prevent itching. Our discussion here pertains to the use of antihistamines for treating only the common cold and allergic rhinitis.

When an allergic reaction occurs, the body releases a chemical called **histamine.** Increased levels of histamine produce reactions that lead to an inflammatory response. This response most often occurs in the nose, because it is so highly vascular.

Antihistamines block this sequence of events, which in turn reduces the amount of nasal secretion. Ultimately, relieving the symptoms of a runny nose.

The most predominant and often bothersome side effect of using antihistamines is **drowsiness.** Some people are more sensitive than others to the drowsiness caused by antihistamines. If sedation is severe or intolerable, contact your physician. There are prescription antihistamines that have no or very little sedating properties. Labeling on OTC antihistamine products provides a warning that says, in effect, "When you use any antihistamine, you should avoid activities and occupations which require alertness," particularly driving a car or operating heavy machinery.

The degree of sedation or drowsiness you experience varies, depending on the antihistamine itself. The most heavily sedating antihistamines are those which contain the ingredients **diphenhydramine** or **clemastine.** The least sedating antihistamines that are available over-the-counter are those containing **pheniramine, brompheniramime, chlorpheniramine,** and **triprolidine.** The ingredient **pyrilamine** has an intermediate or moderate sedation effect in comparison with the others.

In addition, the effects of sedation you experience will be exaggerated when antihistamines are taken along with other products containing alcohol, sedatives, hypnotics, antidepressants, antipsychotics, certain analgesics, and anti-anxiety agents.

Decongestants

Decongestants relieve nasal stuffiness by constricting the blood vessels in the nasal mucosa. This reduces the enlargement (or engorgement) of the mucous membranes and consequently promotes nasal ventilation, drainage, and relief from stuffiness.

Decongestants are available in both **topical** and **oral** forms. Topical nasal decongestants are administered either as sprays or drops.

Caution: When you select a topical nasal decongestant for self-treatment of allergic rhinitis, you want to be sure to limit your use of it to three days to prevent something known as **rebound congestion.** As the name implies, rebound congestion is severe congestion caused by the excessive or abusive use of topical nasal decongestants. Many people become "addicted" to the nasal decongestants and, in an effort to relieve the rebound congestion that results, begin using the products excessively. The consequences of this condition are serious and can be dangerous. A physician *should* be consulted. Do not overuse these or any medications.

Prior to administering sprays or drops, gently blow the nose to help rid the nasal passages of as much secretion as possible.

Use a **nasal spray** with your head in an upright position, and follow three to five minutes later by blowing the nose. This three to five minute waiting period is important. It gives the medication time to start working.

Unlike nasal sprays, you should administer **nasal drops** into the lower nostril opening while you are in a reclining position. Remain in this position for about five minutes to assure proper absorption, then repeat the process for the other nostril.

When you select a topical nasal decongestant, you will want to consider both the duration of its effect and ease of usage. Some topical products are designed as short-acting products while others are long-acting. In other words, one product may be intended to be used every four hours while others are to be used every 12 hours. This may be very important to you if your dosing schedule is not flexible.

Typically, decongestants taken orally last longer than sprays and drops; however, they take longer to act. Rebound congestion is not a problem with oral decongestants, because they do not come in direct contact with the nasal mucosa as do sprays or drops.

Plan to limit your usage of oral nasal decongestants to no more than ten days. If further use seems warranted, you need to consult a physician.

When selecting an oral nasal decongestant, consider the dosage form (liquid or tablet), how long it takes before the decongestant becomes effective, and how long the benefits last.

As with all medications, you should always read the package label for any cautions or warnings regarding who should not use the particular product. People with high blood pressure, diabetes, heart disease, or overactive thyroid should take oral decongestants *only* with the advice of a physician.

Expectorants

Coughs are either **productive**, that is, producing **phlegm**, or **non-productive.** Nonproductive coughs are dry and hacking.

You should use an expectorant to treat a productive cough. **Water** is the best expectorant. In fact, a well-hydrated body involving no medication enhances expectoration. It is always a good idea to drink lots of water unless your physician has placed you on a fluid-restricted diet. In general, you should greatly increase your consumption of fluids especially when a productive cough is present.

Some OTC cough-and-cold medications contain expectorants. At this time, however, **guaifenesin** is the only expectorant that is classified as "safe and effective" by the FDA Advisory Panel. See Table 1-3 (page 23).

Anti-tussives

Note: Do not use anti-tussives when congestion or phlegm is present.

Use an anti-tussive to treat a cough that is nonproductive, dry, or hacking.

Anti-tussives help decrease the frequency of a cough. Increasing air humidity is another way to help decrease the frequency of a cough. Many people find a steam or cool mist vaporizer to be very helpful.

If a nonproductive cough persists for more than ten (10) days, consult your physician to rule out possible complications.

Analgesics

Analgesics relieve fever, sore throat or eyes, headaches or general body aches.

Tylenol™ (acetaminophen) is the most common analgesic in OTC cold and allergy preparations. **Aspirin** and **ibuprofen** are also common, but may cause stomach distress.

Aspirin has been associated with **Reye's Syndrome,** a sudden loss of consciousness which may result in death. Therefore, you want to avoid aspirin when the flu, chicken pox, or other viral infections are present or possible.

Single Versus Multiple Symptoms

If you show signs of a **single** symptom, such as increased nasal secretion, you want to select a medication that contains only an antihistamine. You should not select a medication that treats **multiple** symptoms.

Whenever possible, it is best to use a single-symptom OTC medication when a single symptom exists. However, if you do have multiple symptoms, try to locate and select an OTC product that treats *all* of your symptoms specifically.

Several single-symptom products may be used together. However, this is often more expensive than selecting and using one multi-symptom product.

Remember, when you make your OTC product selection, you want to keep in mind dosing schedules, dosage form (liquid, tablet, capsule, etc.), price, and any warnings that appear on the medication packaging itself.

As with any OTC medication, choose cold or allergy medications wisely. If you are pregnant or have elevated blood pressure, heart arrhythmias, diabetes, or an overactive thyroid, be certain to exercise extreme caution. If you are not sure about which OTC medication to use, always consult your Eckerd Pharmacist or your physician.

Use the key below to reference the remaining tables in this chapter that include multi-source products.

Key to Common Multi-Source, Multi-Symptom Products

Decon-gestants	Antihista-mine	Analgesic	Expect-orant	Anti-tussive	Table	Page
●		●			1-6	27
●	●				1-7	28
●	●	●			1-8	30
●			●		1-9	32
●				●	1-10	33
●	●			●	1-11	34
●	●	●		●	1-12	35
●		●		●	1-13	37
●			●	●	1-14	38
●		●	●	●	1-15	39
			●	●	1-16	40

New Product Update!

Recently, a medication that was previously available only by prescription, changed to an over-the-counter status. This product is Nasalcrom™.

Nasalcrom™ is a nasal solution used to prevent and treat symptoms of allergic rhinitis. If relief is not seen within two (2) weeks of use, discontinue Nasalcrom™. When treating seasonal rhinitis, avoidance of the allergens will greatly improve the effects of treatment. Treatment should be continued throughout the exposure period. When treating perennial rhinitis, two (2) to four (4) weeks of treatment may be necessary. Initially, the addition of antihistamines or decongestants may be necessary; however, these additional products should be discontinued once improvement is seen. Do not use Nasalcrom™ for more than 12 weeks unless so instructed by your physician. The most common side effects experienced with the use of Nasalcrom™ include sneezing, nasal stinging, and nasal burning. If you need more information on this new over-the-counter product, please talk to your Eckerd Pharmacist.

TABLE 1-1: Common Single-Source OTC Antihistamines

Generic Name	National Brand Products	Eckerd Brand Products	Dosage Form(s)
Chlorphenira-mine Maleate	Chlor-Trimeton 4 Hour Allergy	Allergy Relief Tablets	Tablet
Bromphenira-mine Maleate	Dimetapp Allergy	Brom-tapp (Tablets, Elixir)	Tablet, Elixir, Liqui-gel
	Dimetapp Allergy Extentabs	Brom-tapp Extend (Tablets)	Tablet-Time Released
Diphenhydra-mine Hydrochloride	Benadryl	Diphedryl Elixir	Elixir
	Benadryl 25	Diphedryl (Tablet) and Healthline Anti-histamine Pink	Tablet, Capsule
	Benadryl Dye Free	Diphedryl Dye Free	Liquid
Clemastine Fumarate	Contac 12-Hour Allergy	Clemastine-1	Tablet
	Tavist-1	Clemastine-1	Tablet

TABLE 1-2: Common Single-Source OTC Decongestants

Generic Name	National Brand Products	Eckerd Brand Products	Dosage Form(s)
Pseudoephed-rine Hydrochloride	Chlor-trimeton Non-Drowsy 4-Hour		Tablet
	Dimetapp Decongestant Non-Drowsy		Liqui-gel
	Dimetapp Decongestant Pediatric		Drops
	Drixoral Non-Drowsy Formula		Tablet-Time Released
	Non-Drowsy Sudafed Decongestant (Children & Infant)		Chewable Tablet, Liquid
	Pediacare Infant's Decongestant	Infant's Nasal Decongestant Drops	Drops
	Sudafed	Su-phedrin	Tablet
	Sudafed 12-Hour		Tablet-Time Released
	Sudafed 12-Hour Caplet		Caplet-Time Released
	Sudafed Children's		Liquid
	Triaminic AM Decongestant Formula		Liquid
	Triaminic Infant's Oral Decongestant		Drops

continued

TABLE 1-2: Common Single-Source OTC Decongestants (continued)

Generic Name	National Brand Products	Eckerd Brand Products	Dosage Form(s)
Phenylephrine Hydrochloride & Naphazoline Hydrochloride	4-Way Fast Acting		Nasal Spray
Oxymetazoline Hydrochloride	4-Way Long Lasting		Nasal Spray
	Afrin 12-Hour	Decongestant Nasal Spray 12-Hour	Nasal Spray, Drops, Pump
	Afrin 12-Hour Pediatric		Nasal Drops
	Afrin Extra Moisturizing	Extra Moisturizing Sinus Spray	Nasal Spray
	Afrin Sinus	Moisturizing Sinus Spray (12-Hour)	Nasal Spray
	Allerest		Nasal Spray
	Benzedrex 12-Hour		Nasal Spray
	Dristan 12-Hour		Nasal Spray
	Duration		Nasal Spray, Pump
	Neo-Synephrine Maximum 12-Hour		Nasal Spray
	Vicks Sinex 12- Hour		Nasal Spray
Phenylephrine Hydrochloride	Dristan		Nasal Spray

continued

TABLE 1-2: Common Single-Source OTC Decongestants (continued)

Generic Name	National Brand Products	Eckerd Brand Products	Dosage Form(s)
	Neo-Syneprhine Extra		Nasal Spray, Drops
	Neo-Synephrine Mild		Nasal Spray
	Neo-Synephrine Pediatric		Nasal Drops
	Neo-Synephrine Regular		Nasal Spray, Drops, Pump
	Sinex Regular		Nasal Spray
	Vicks Sinus		Nasal Spray
Propylhexa-drine	Benzedrex (menthol)		Nasal Inhaler
Levodesoxy-ephedrine	Vicks Vapor Inhaler	Decongestant Inhaler	Nasal Inhaler

TABLE 1-3: Common Single-Source OTC Expectorants

Generic Name	National Brand Products	Eckerd Brand Products	Dosage Form(s)
Guafenesin	Naldecon Senior EX		Liquid
	Robitussin	Tussin	Syrup

TABLE 1-4: Common Single Source OTC Anti-tussives

Generic Name	National Brand Products	Eckerd Brand Products	Dosage Form(s)
Dextro-methorphan	Benylin Pediatric Cough Formula		Liquid
	Delsym Extended Release		Suspension
	Formula 44 Cough Mixture		Liquid
	Formula 44 Pediatric Cough Medicine		Liquid
	Robitussin Pediatric Cough		Liquid
	Vicks 44 Dry Hacking Cough		Liquid

Remember: After selecting the OTC medication-type that most accurately treats your symptoms, it is important to consider which product is best for you. Although the same active ingredients may be found in several drugs, the amount contained per dose may differ. This can affect the dosing schedule needed to treat your symptoms adequately. If you have restrictions to or allergies to alcohol, sugar, or sodium, check the contents to ensure safety. If you are uncertain, please contact your Eckerd Pharmacist or physician.

TABLE 1-5: Common Single-Source OTC Analgesics

Generic Name	National Brand Products	Eckerd Brand Products	Dosage Form(s)
Acetaminophen	Feverall Junior Strength		Tablet, Suppository
	Tempra 1 Drops		Drops
	Tempra 2 Syrup		Syrup
	Tylenol Children's	Children's Non-Aspirin Fever & Pain Reliever	Elixir
	Tylenol Children's	Children's Non-Aspirin Fever & Pain Reliever	Suspension
	Tylenol Children's	Children's Non-Aspirin Fever & Pain Reliever	Chewable Tablet
	Tylenol Extra Strength Adult Liquid Pain Reliever		Liquid
	Tylenol Extra Strength	Extra Strength Pain Relief	Tablet
	Tylenol Extra Strength Headache Plus	Extra Strength Pain Relief	Caplet
	Tylenol Extra Strength	Extra Strength Pain Relief	Tablet
	Tylenol Infant's	Infant's Non-Aspirin Fever & Pain Relief	Drops
	Tylor Jr. Strength (regular and chewable)	Jr. Strength Non-Aspirin Fever & Pain Reliever	Caplet, Chewable Tablet
	Tylenol Regular Strength		Tablet, Gelcap, Capsule

continued

◀ 25

TABLE 1-5: Common Single-Source OTC Analgesics (continued)

Generic Name	National Brand Products	Eckerd Brand Products	Dosage Form(s)
Aspirin	Alka-Seltzer with Aspirin Extra Strength		Effervescent Tablet
	Alka-Seltzer with Aspirin (original)		Effervescent Tablet
	Anacin	Adult Strength Aspirin	Tablet
	Bayer (original)	Thin Coat Aspirin	Tablet, Caplet
	Bayer Extra Strength		Tablet, Caplet
	Bayer Children's Aspirin	Children's Aspirin	Tablet, Chewable Tablet
	BC		Powder
	Bufferin	Buffered Aspirin	Tablet, Caplet
	Stanback		Powder
Ibuprofen	Advil	Ibuprofen	Tablet, Caplet
	Advil Children's		Suspension
	Motrin IB	Ibuprofen	Tablet, Caplet
	Motrin Children's		Suspension, Chewable Tablet
	Nuprin	Ibuprofen	Tablet, Caplet
	Aleve	Naproxen	Tablet, Caplet
Naproxen	Actron		Tablet
Ketoprofen	Orudis KT		Tablet

TABLE 1-6: Common Multi-Symptom Decongestant/Analgesic OTC Products

National Brand Products	Eckerd Brand Products	Decongestant	Analgesic	Dosage Form(s)
Advil Cold & Sinus		Pseudoephed-rine	Ibuprofen	Tablet, Caplet
Dristan Cold Maximum Strength No Drowsiness		Pseudoephed-rine	Acetaminophen	Gelcap
Dristan Sinus		Pseudoephed-rine	Ibuprofen	Caplet
Motrin IB Sinus		Pseudoephed-rine	Ibuprofen	Tablet, Caplet
Sinarest No Drowsiness		Pseudoephed-rine	Acetaminophen	Tablet
Sinutab	Sinus Headache Tablets	Pseudoephed-rine	Acetaminophen	Tablet
Sinutab Maximum Strength without Drowsiness	Max Strength Sinus Headache	Pseudoephed-rine	Acetaminophen	Tablet, Caplet
Sudafed Sinus	Su-phedrin Sinus	Pseudoephed-rine	Acetaminophen	Tablet, Caplet
Tylenol Sinus Maximum Strength	Maximum Strength Non-Aspirin Sinus Relief	Pseudoephed-rine	Acetaminophen	Tablet, Gelcap
Vicks Dayquil Sinus Pressure & Pain Relief		Pseudoephed-rine	Ibuprofen	Caplet

TABLE 1-7: Common Multi-Symptom Decongestant/Antihistimine OTC Products

National Brand Products	Eckerd Brand Products	Decongestant	Antihistamine	Dosage Form(s)
Actifed	A-phedrin (Tablets only)	Pseudoephed-rine	Triprolidine	Tablet, Syrup
Actifed Allergy Daytime/ Nighttime		Daytime & Nighttime: Pseudoephed-rine	Nighttime only: Diphenhy-dramine	Caplet
Allerest Maximum Strength		Pseudoephed-rine	Chlorpheni-ramine	Tablet
Benadryl Allergy Decongestant Medication		Pseudoephed-rine	Diphenhy-dramine	Liquid
Benadryl D		Pseudoephed-rine	Diphenhy-dramine	Tablet, Capsule
Chlor-Trimeton 12-Hour Allergy Decongestant		Pseudoephed-rine	Chlorphe-niramine	Tablet
Chlor-Trimeton 4-Hour Allergy Decongestant		Pseudoephed-rine	Chlorphe-niramine	Tablet
Contac 12-Hour Cold	Cold Capsules	Phenylpro-panolamine	Chlorphe-niramine	Capsule-Time Released
Dimetapp		Phenylpro-panolamine	Bromphe-niramine	Elixir
Dimetapp Cold & Allergy		Phenylpro-panolamine	Bromphe-niramine	Chew-able Tablet, Quick Dissolve Tablets

continued

TABLE 1-7: Common Multi-Symptom Decongestant/ Antihistimine OTC Products (continued)

National Brand Products	Eckerd Brand Products	Decongestant	Antihistamine	Dosage Form(s)
Dimetapp Maximum Strength 12-Hour Extentabs	Brom-tapp 12-Hour	Phenylpro-panolamine	Bromphe-niramine	Tablet-Time Released
Dimetapp Maximum Strength 4-Hour		Phenylpro-panolamine	Bromphniramine	Tablet, Liqui-gel
Drixoral Cold & Allergy Sustained-Release	12-Hour Anti-histamine Nasal Decongestant	Pseudoephed-rine	Dexbrom-pheniramine	Tablet-Time Released
Pediacare Cold Allergy for ages 6–12		Pseudoephed-rine	Chlorphe-niramine	Chewable Tablet
Sudafed Cold And Allergy	Su-phedrin Nasal Decon-gestant plus Antihistamine	Pseudoephed-rine	Chlorphe-niramine	Tablet
Tavist-D	Clemastine + D	Phenylpro-panolamine	Clemastine	Tablet
Triaminic Cold & Allergy	Tri-Acting (Orange Flavor)	Phenylpro-panolamine	Chlorphe-niramine	Syrup

TABLE 1-8: Common Multi-Symptom Decongestant/ Antihistamine/Analgesic OTC Products

National Brand Products	Eckerd Brand Products	Decongestant	Antihistamine	Analgesic	Dosage Form(s)
Actifed Plus		Pseudoephed-rine	Triprolidine	Acetaminophen	Tablet, Caplet
Actifed Sinus Daytime/ Nighttime		Daytime & Nighttime: Pseudoephed-rine	Nighttime only: Diphenhydra-mine	Daytime & Nighttime: Acetaminophen	Tablet, Caplet
Alka-Seltzer Plus Cold Medicine	Effervescent Cold Medicine	Phenylpro-panolamine	Chlorphenir-amine	Aspirin	Effervescent Tablet
Alka-Seltzer Plus Cold Medicine Liqui-Gels	Cold Medicine Liqui-Cap	Pseudoephed-rine	Chlorphenir-amine	Acetaminophen	Softgels
Alka-Seltzer Plus Maximum Strength Sinus Medicine		Phenylpro-panolamine	Bromphenir-amine	Aspirin	Powder
Benadryl Allergy Sinus Headache Formula	Diphedryl Allergy/Sinus/ Head	Pseudoephed-rine	Diphenhydra-mine	Acetaminophen	Tablet
Contac Day & Night Allergy/Sinus		Daytime & Nighttime: Pseudoephed-rine	Nighttime only: Diphenhydra-mine	Acetaminophen	Caplet
Coricidin D		Phenylpro-panolamine	Chlorphenir-amine	Acetaminophen	Tablet
Dimetapp Cold & Flu		Phenylpro-panolamine	Bromphenir-amine	Acetaminophen	Caplet
Dristan Cold Multi-Sympt.	Decongestant Cold Tablets	Phenylephrine	Chlorphenir-amine	Acetaminophen	Tablet

continued

TABLE 1-8: Common Multi-Symptom Decongestant/ Antihistamine/Analgesic OTC Products (continued)

National Brand Products	Eckerd Brand Products	Decongestant	Antihistamine	Analgesic	Dosage Form(s)
Drixoral Cold & Flu		Pseudoephed-rine	Dexbromphe-niramine	Acetaminophen	Tablet-Time Released
Sinutab Sinus Allergy Medication	Sinus Head-ache (Sinus, Congestion, Pressure)	Pseudoephed-rine	Chlorphen-iramine	Acetaminophen	Tablet, Caplet
TheraFlu Flu and Cold Medicine	Flu & Cold Packets	Pseudoephed-rine	Chlorphen-iramine	Acetaminophen	Powder Packet
Triaminicin		Phenylpro-panolamine	Chlorphen-iramine	Acetaminophen	Tablet
Tylenol Allergy Sinus Maximum Strength	Non-Aspirin Allergy/Sinus Relief	Pseudoephed-rine	Chlorphen-iramine	Acetaminophen	Caplet, Gelcap
Tylenol Allergy Sinus Nighttime Maximum Strength	Non-Aspirin Night Allergy/Sinus Relief	Pseudoephed-rine	Diphenhy-dramine	Acetaminophen	Caplet
Tylenol Children s Cold Multi-Symptom		Pseudoephed-rine	Chlorphen-iramine	Acetaminophen	Chewable Tablet, Liquid
Tylenol Cold Nighttime		Pseudoephed-rine	Diphenhy-dramine	Acetaminophen	Liquid
Tylenol Flu Night Time Max Strength		Pseudoephed-rine	Diphenhy-dramine	Acetaminophen	Gelcap

TABLE 1-9: Common Multi-Symptom Decongestant/Expectorant OTC Products

National Brand Products	Eckerd Brand Products	Decongestant	Expectorant	Dosage Form(s)
Naldecon EX Children's		Phenylpro-panolamine	Guaifenesin	Syrup
Naldecon EX Pediatric		Phenylpro-panolamine	Guaifenesin	Drops
Robitussin PE	Tussin PE	Pseudoephed-rine	Guaifenesin	Syrup
Robitussin Severe Congestion Liqui-Gels	Tussin Severe Congestion Liqui-gels	Pseudoephed-rine	Guaifenesin	Softgel
Sinutab Non-Drying		Pseudoephed-rine	Guaifenesin	Liqui-cap
Triaminic Expectorant	Tri-Acting (Citrus)	Phenylpro-panolamine	Guaifenesin	Liquid
Vicks Dayquil Sinus Pressure & Congestion Relief		Phenylpro-panolamine	Guaifenesin	Caplet

TABLE 1-10: Common Multi-Symptom Decongestant/Anti-tussive OTC Products

National Brand Products	Eckerd Brand Products	Decongestant	Anti-tussive	Dosage Form(s)
Robitussin Maximum Strength Cough & Cold	Tussin Maximum Strength Cough & Cold	Pseudoephed-rine	Dextro-methorphan	Liquid
Triaminic AM Cough & Decongestant Formula		Pseudoephed-rine	Dextro-methorphan	Liquid
Triaminic-DM Syrup		Phenylpro-panolamine	Dextro-methorphan	Liquid
Vicks 44 Dry Hacking Cough & Head Congestion		Pseudoephed-rine	Dextro-methorphan	Liquid
Vicks 44 Pediatric Dry Hacking Cough & Head Congestion		Pseudoephed-rine	Dextro-methorphan	Liquid

TABLE 1-11: Common Multi-Symptom Decongestant/ Antihistamine/Anti-tussive OTC Products

National Brand Products	Eckerd Brand Products	Decongestant	Antihistamine	Anti-tussive	Dosage Form(s)
Dimetapp Cold & Cough Maximum Strength		Phenylpropanolamine	Brompheniramine	Dextromethorphan	Liqui-gel
Dimetapp DM		Phenylpropanolamine	Brompheniramine	Dextromethorphan	Liquid
Nyquil Children's Cold/Cough Medicine	Children's Nighttime Cough and Cold Formula	Pseudoephedrine	Chlorpheniramine	Dextromethorphan	Liquid
Pediacare Cough-Cold Formula	Pediatric Cough & Cold Formula	Pseudoephedrine	Chlorpheniramine	Dextromethorphan	Liquid
Pediacare Cough-Cold for Ages 6 to 12		Pseudoephedrine	Chlorpheniramine	Dextromethorphan	Chewable Tablet
Robitussin Pediatric Night Relief		Pseudoephedrine	Chlorpheniramine	Dextromethorphan	Liquid
Triaminic Nite Time Maximum Strength		Pseudoephedrine	Chlorpheniramine	Dextromethorphan	Liquid
Triaminicol Multi-Symptom Cold		Phenylpropanolamine	Chlorpheniramine	Dextromethorphan	Tablet
Triaminicol Multi-Symptom Relief		Phenylpropanolamine	Chlorpheniramine	Dextromethorphan	Liquid
Vicks 44M Pediatric Cough & Cold Relief		Pseudoephedrine	Chlorpheniramine	Dextromethorphan	Liquid

TABLE 1-12: Common Multi-Symptom Decongestant/Antihistamine/Analgesic/ Anti-tussive OTC Products

National Brand Products	Eckerd Brand Products	Decon-gestant	Antihista-mine	Analgesic	Anti-tussive	Dosage Form(s)
Alka-Seltzer Plus Cold and Cough Medicine		Phenylpro-panolamine	Chlorphenir-amine	Aspirin	Dextromth-orphan	Effervescent Tablet
Alka-Seltzer Plus Cough & Cold Liqui-gel		Pseudo-ephedrine	Chlorphenir-amine	Aceta-minophen	Dextromth-orphan	Softgel
Alka-Seltzer Plus Night-time Cold Medicine		Phenylpro-panolamine	Brompheni-ramine	Aspirin	Dextromth-orphan	Effervescent Tablet
Alka-Seltzer Plus Night-time Cold Liqui-gel		Pseudo-ephedrine	Doxylamine	Aceta-minophen	Dextromth-orphan	Softgel
Comtrex Max Strength		Pseudo-ephedrine	Chlorphenir-amine	Aceta-minophen	Dextromth-orphan	Tablet, Caplet, Liquid
Comtrex Max Strength	Maximum Strength Multi-Symptom Cold	Phenylpro-panolamine	Chlorphenir-amine	Aceta-minophen	Dextromth-orphan	Liqui-gel
Comtrex Max Strength Day & Night		Datyime & Nighttime: Pseudo-ephedrine	Nighttime only: Chlorphenir-amine	Day & Night: Aceta-minophen	Day & Night: Dextro-methorphan	Day: Caplet Night: Tablet
Contac Day & Night Cold/Flu		Day & Night: Pseudo-ephedrine	Night only: Diphenhy-dramine	Day & Night: Aceta-minophen	Day only: Dextro-methorphan	Day & Night: Caplet
Contac Severe Cold & Flu Non-Drowsy	Severe Cold	Phenylpro-panolamine	Chlorphenir-amine	Aceta-minophen	Dextro-methorphan	Caplet
Robitussin Night Relief		Pseudo-ephedrine	Pyrilamine	Aceta-minophen	Dextro-methorphan	Liquid
TheraFlu Max Strength Nighttime		Pseudo-ephedrine	Chlorphenir-amine	Aceta-minophen	Dextro-methorphan	Powder Packet
TheraFlu, Flu Cold & Cough	Flu, Cold and Cough Hot Liquid Medicine	Pseudo-ephedrine	Chlorphenir-amine	Aceta-minophen	Dextro-methorphan	Powder Packet

continued

TABLE 1-12: Common Multi-Symptom Decongestant/ Antihistamine/Analgesic/Anti-tussive OTC Products (continued)

National Brand Products	Eckerd Brand Products	Decon-gestant	Antihista-mine	Analgesic	Anti-tussive	Dosage Form(s)
Tylenol Children's Multi-Symptom Plus Cough	Children's Multi-Symptom Cold	Pseudo-ephedrine	Chlorphenir-amine	Acetamin-ophen	Dextro-methorphan	Liquid
Tylenol Children's Cold Plus Cough		Pseudo-ephedrine	Chlorphenir-amine	Acetamin-ophen	Dextro-methorphan	Chewable Tablet
Tylenol Cold & Flu Hot Medication		Pseudo-ephedrine	Chlorphenir-amine	Acetamin-ophen	Dextro-methorphan	Powder Packet
Tylenol Multi-Symptom Cold		Pseudo-ephedrine	Chlorphenir-amine	Acetamin-ophen	Dextro-methorphan	Caplet
Vicks 44M Cough Cold & Flu Relief		Pseudo-ephedrine	Chlorphenir-amine	Acetamin-ophen	Dextro-methorphan	Liquid
Vicks NyQuil Hot Therapy		Pseudo-ephedrine	Doxylamine	Acetamin-ophen	Dextro-methorphan	Powder Packet

TABLE 1-13: Common Multi-Symptom Decongestant/Analgesic/Anti-tussive OTC Products

National Brand Products	Eckerd Brand Products	Decon-gestant	Analgesic	Anti-tussive	Dosage Form(s)
Comtrex Max Strength Non-Drowsy Caplet		Pseudo-ephedrine	Aceta-minophen	Dextrometh-orphan	Caplet
Comtrex Max Strength Non-Drowsy		Phenylpro-panolamine	Aceta-minophen	Dextrometh-orphan	Liqui-gel
Thera Flu Max Strength Non-Drowsy		Pseudo-ephedrine	Aceta-minophen	Dextrometh-orphan	Caplet
Triaminic Sore Throat Formula		Pseudo-ephedrine	Aceta-minophen	Dextrometh-orphan	Liquid
Tylenol Cold No Drowsiness Formula	Non-Drowsy Non-Aspirin Multi-Symptom Cold	Pseudo-ephedrine	Aceta-minophen	Dextrometh-orphan	Caplet, Gelcap
Tylenol Cold & Flu Hot Medication No Drowsiness		Pseudo-ephedrine	Aceta-minophen	Dextrometh-orphan	Powder Packet
Tylenol Flu Max-Strength	Maximum Strength Non-Aspirin Multi-Symptom Flu Relief	Pseudo-ephedrine	Aceta-minophen	Dextrometh-orphan	Gelcap
Tylenol Multi-Symptom Cough with Decongestant		Pseudo-ephedrine	Aceta-minophen	Dextrometh-orphan	Liquid

TABLE 1-14: Common Multi-Source Decongestant/ Expectorant/Anti-Tussive OTC Products

National Brand Products	Eckerd Brand Products	Decon-gestant	Expectorant	Anti-tussive	Dosage Form(s)
Benylin Multi-Symptom Cough Formula		Pseudo-ephedrine	Guaifenesin	Dextrometh-orphan	Liquid
Naldecon DX (Adult, Children & Pediatric)		Phenylpro-panolamine	Guaifenesin	Dextrometh-orphan	Liquid, Drops, Syrup
Robitussin CF	Tussin CF	Phenylpro-panolamine	Guaifenesin	Dextrometh-orphan	Liquid
Robitussin Cold & Cough Liqui-Gels	Tussin Cough & Cold Relief	Pseudo-ephedrine	Guaifenesin	Dextrometh-orphan	Softgel
Sudafed Cold and Cough	Su-Phedrin Cough and Cold	Pseudo-ephedrine	Guaifenesin	Dextrometh-orphan	Liqui-gels

TABLE 1-15: Common Multi-Symptom Decongestant/ Analgesic/Expectorant/Anti-tussive OTC Products

National Brand Products	Eckerd Brand Products	Decon-gestant	Analgesic	Expec-torant	Anti-tussive	Dosage Form(s)
Sudafed Cold & Cough Liquid Caps	Su-phedrine Cough & Cold	Pseudo-ephedrine	Acetamin-ophen	Guaifen-esin	Dextrometh-orphan	Capsule
Vicks DayQuil Multi-Symptom Cold/Flu Relief		Pseudo-ephedrine	Acetamin-ophen	Guaifen-esin	Dextrometh-orphan	Liquid

38 ❯

TABLE 1-16: Common Multi-Symptom Expectorant/Anti-Tussive OTC Products

National Brand Products	Eckerd Brand Products	Expectorant	Anti-tussive	Dosage Form(s)
Benylin Expectorant Cough Formula		Guaifenesin	Dextromethorphan	Liquid
Diabetic Tussin DM	Tussin DM	Guaifenesin	Dextromethorphan	Liquid, Gelcaps
Naldecon Senior DX		Guaifenesin	Dextromethorphan	Liquid
Robitussin DM	Tussin DM	Guaifenesin	Dextromethorphan	Liquid
Vicks 44e Chest Cough & Chest Congestion		Guaifenesin	Dextromethorphan	Liquid
Vicks 44e Pediatric Chest Cough & Chest Congestion		Guaifenesin	Dextromethorphan	Liquid

It's right at Eckerd!

One of the ways that it's right at Eckerd is when it comes to the ease and efficiency of your prescription refills. Have your prescription number ready, then call your Eckerd Pharmacy about 24 hours in advance of when you need your prescription. When you come in the next day, your prescription is ready for you—no waiting.

Here's an interesting fact about generic brands: When it comes to generic brands, you can save up to 50 percent on your prescriptions at your Eckerd Pharmacy and, at the same time, help do your part to keep your plan premiums down. We approve only generics of the highest quality—those which match the name-brand drugs for both safety and effectiveness. Ask your Eckerd Pharmacist if an Eckerd-approved generic is available for your prescription.

Remember, your Eckerd Pharmacist is always available to provide personal counseling about your medications and to talk about the health issues that are important to you.

Get updates to the information in this book at the **Eckerd Corporation Home Page** on the World Wide Web. Visit us often at **www.eckerd.com.**

Chapter Two

Choosing the Proper Pain or Fever-Relieving Product

2

Many over-the-counter (OTC) pain-relieving **(analgesic)** and fever-relieving **(anti-pyretic)** products are currently available. Choosing the best product can often be confusing and difficult. The key to treating pain or fever successfully is to identify your symptoms and be educated as to the type of medication that will provide the best relief. The OTC analgesic and anti-pyretic products that are currently available contain aspirin (or aspirin-like ingredients), acetaminophen, ibuprofen, naproxen, or ketoprofen.

OTC Analgesic and Fever-Relieving Product Ingredients and Their Side Effects

Aspirin

Aspirin is effective in treating fever and mild to moderate pain due to headache, muscle pain, arthritis, menstruation, and swelling due to inflammation. Often, higher doses than what are recommended for OTC use are necessary to produce **anti-inflammatory** or anti-swelling effects. For this reason, ibuprofen, ketoprofen, or naproxen may provide more relief of pain associated with arthritis or long-term muscle pain.

Aspirin should not be used if a person has a bleeding disorder, stomach ulcer disease, chicken pox, or a history of gout or hyperuricemia (excessive uric acid), or by patients who are allergic to tartrazine dye or aspirin itself.

The most common symptoms reported with aspirin allergies include hives, difficulty breathing, itching, and swelling. If you experience any of these symptoms after taking aspirin, discontinue its use, and alert your physician(s) and Eckerd Pharmacist.

Do not take aspirin before or after **surgery** because it decreases the blood's ability to clot, causing excessive bleeding.

The most common complaint associated with the use of aspirin is **upset stomach.** For this reason, aspirin may be taken with food or milk. **Enteric-coated** aspirin was designed to reduce the stomach distress that plain aspirin can cause. However, this coating actually delays the absorption of the medication, and thus, the fever or pain relieving effects take longer to be seen. Enteric-coated products should not be used when prompt fever or pain relief is desired.

The use of aspirin has been associated with **Reye's Syndrome,** a sudden loss of consciousness which may result in death. It should not be given to children who have symptoms of a **viral flu** (see Chapter 1 for symptoms), or who have chickenpox.

Aspirin products are available in many forms including tablets (plain, enteric-coated, buffered), suppositories, and effervescent tablets.

Effervescent tablets are associated with fewer GI or gastrointestinal side effects than plain aspirin, but they often have a **high sodium content.** They should be avoided if you are on a sodium-restricted diet or have an illness or disease that warrants restricted sodium levels.

Acetaminophen

Acetaminophen is effective in treating fever or mild to moderate pain associated with headache or other minor aches and pain. It has no significant anti-inflammatory effects and **should not be used** to treat the swelling associated with arthritis, swelling such as a sprained ankle, or muscle pain. However, some physicians are finding that acetaminophen given at specific doses may prove beneficial in **easing the symptom** of pain associated with **osteoarthritis.** Ask your physician or Eckerd Pharmacist about what medications are best for you prior to self-medicating.

Acetaminophen should not be taken if you have **liver disease** or are allergic to acetaminophen. The risk of allergic reaction associated with the use of acetaminophen in patients who are allergic to aspirin is small. Therefore, most people who are allergic to aspirin are able to tolerate acetaminophen.

Products that contain acetaminophen are often chosen over the other analgesic products to relieve headache or anti-fever preparations, since acetaminophen has fewer reported side effects on the stomach than aspirin, ibuprofen, ketoprofen, or naproxen.

Patients who require an analgesic or anti-pyretic, but who have a blood clotting disorder, stomach ulcer disease, chicken pox, viral flu, or patients with a history of gout or hyperuricemia (excessive uric acid), are able to take acetaminophen as an alternative to aspirin, ibuprofen, ketoprofen, or naproxen.

Ibuprofen, Ketoprofen, and Naproxen

Available only by prescription until recently, **ibuprofen, keto-profen,** and **naproxen** are now available in over-the-counter strengths. Products containing these ingredients are very useful when treating symptoms such as headache, muscle ache, arthritis, swelling due to inflammation, menstrual pain, and fever.

Ibuprofen, ketoprofen, and naproxen are considered more potent as analgesics than either aspirin or acetaminophen. Also, these products exhibit better anti-inflammatory effects than aspirin when taken at non-prescription doses. Patients who are allergic to aspirin should not take these products because they may possibly be allergic to these products as well.

Commonly reported side effects with the use of a product containing either ibuprofen, ketoprofen, or naproxen include stomach distress, bleeding of the stomach lining (less significance than with aspirin), nausea, vomiting, and dizziness. To lessen the possible GI or gastrointestinal side effects, these products should be taken with food or milk.

A physician should be notified if **skin rash, itching, visual disturbances, weight gain, black stools,** or **water retention** occurs.

Patients with **renal function impairment, congestive heart failure, diabetes,** or other chronic illness or disease should **not self-medicate** with these products.

Identifying and Treating Pain

Pain is perceived differently by every individual. What one person may consider "intolerable" in regard to pain may merely be classified as "uncomfortable" by another. OTC and prescription medications are quite effective in relieving pain.

When treating pain, it is very important to determine where the pain is coming from, how often and when it occurs, how long it lasts, and how severe it is. Pain that **occurs frequently,** or causes **numbness, dizziness, blurred vision, vomiting, nausea, fever,** or **confusion** should **not** be self-treated. If these symptoms occur, contact your physician.

There are four main types of pain that respond well to OTC analgesic products. These include headache, muscle pain, joint pain, and menstrual pain.

Headache

Almost everyone has experienced a headache at least once during their lifetime. Some headaches do not last long and do not need OTC treatment. However, there are times that relief is desired. There are three types of headaches that respond well to OTC analgesics; they include **migraines, sinus,** and **tension** headaches.

Migraine headaches are classified as **common, classic,** or **cluster.** Cluster migraines should be treated only under the care of a physician. Common migraine headaches are generally characterized by sudden headache pain and are accompanied by nausea and vomiting as well as increased sensitivity to light and sound. Classic migraine headaches differ from the other types in that they start with visual disturbances of bright or flashing lights or blind spots as well as difficulty in speaking. They may also be associated with muscle weakness. Both classic or common migraines often respond well to OTC analgesic self-medication.

Sinus headache is common when an infection occurs (as diagnosed by a physician) or when nasal congestion—a symptom of a cold or allergic rhinits—is present. Sinus headaches are generally worse after a night's sleep or nap, but they seem to improve after a while when returning to an upright position. When blockage or congestion is present, it may prove beneficial to place an extra pillow under your head to allow for improved nasal drainage. Oral or nasal decongestants (see Chapter 1) may also relieve some of the symptoms associated with a sinus headache.

Tension headaches are often described as a gradual feeling of tightness on the scalp itself. This tightness may actually worsen to being a bothersome, throbbing feeling. These headaches are often caused by stress and may last for several days. OTC analgesic products are often quite effective for treating these headaches. In addition to OTC therapy, a gentle massage applied to the head or scalp may be beneficial to relieve this pain. If these types of headaches occur frequently or are not relieved by OTC analgesics, consult your physician.

Muscle Pain

Muscle pain is most often due to improper or excessive **exercise.** It can also be caused by certain diseases or infections. This type of pain is associated with **inflammation** and, therefore, responds best to aspirin, ibuprofen, ketoprofen, or naproxen.

In addition to OTC analgesic therapy, the application of **heat** (moist or dry) and/or a soothing **massage** can ease the discomfort associated with muscle pain.

Joint Pain

The most common types of joint pain are found in **osteoarthritis, rheumatoid arthritis,** and **bursitis.** Heat applications to the area of joint pain often eases symptoms. **Inflammation** associated with this type of arthritis responds well to aspirin, ibuprofen, ketoprofen, or naproxen.

Osteoarthritis is characterized by joint stiffness and pain. Some physicians are finding that acetaminophen is beneficial in relieving the pain associated with osteoarthritis. This is because the pain associated with osteoarthritis is not necessarily due to inflammation. If you suspect that you have either type of arthritis, your physician can help you determine the best treatment.

Exercise can greatly decrease symptoms associated with osteoarthritis. Weight-bearing joints found in the hands, hips, knees, and spine are the most affected with osteoarthritis, and the pain can be quite severe. People who are obese may suffer more with osteoarthritis. Weight loss will prove beneficial for these people. Learn all you can about osteoarthritis. Educational materials such as pamphlets, newsletters, and videos are readily available from the Arthritis Foundation.

Rheumatoid arthritis is characterized by joint stiffness and pain, joint swelling, weakness, and muscle pain. The most commonly affected joints include the wrists, hands, fingers, toes, and feet. Joints often become red, swollen, and warm to the touch. Rheumatoid arthritis is often treated initially with aspirin (often at higher doses than is recommended for OTC use), ibuprofen, ketoprofen, or naproxen. However, because it is a **disabling** disease that can get progressively worse, contact your physician and discuss which medication will work best for you. Contact the Arthritis Foundation for educational materials devoted to the topic of rheumatoid arthritis including the latest treatments and findings associated with the disease.

Bursitis most often affects the shoulders, knees, or elbows (tennis elbow). Common symptoms include pain and the inability to move the affected area. To speed recovery, it is best to limit the activity and movement of the joint. OTC analgesic products often provide temporary relief for the pain associated with bursitis.

Menstrual Pain

Although most women do not experience severe pain during menstruation and are able to function normally during this time, this is not true of all women. Some experience pain that is so bothersome that they are unable to go to work or school and are unable to perform simple daily tasks.

Painful or difficult menstruation is called **dysmenorrhea.** The most common complaints include headache, cramping, and lower back pain. The degree of pain experienced by women during menstruation varies greatly. For those women who feel that they need to treat the pain, there are several products from which to choose. All of the OTC analgesics described here will help to ease the pain associated with dysmenorrhea. Ibuprofen, ketoprofen, and naproxen are the drugs of choice for this type of pain. Best results occur when these products are taken on regular schedule, that is, every "x" hours rather than "as needed." If pain persists or worsens, contact your physician.

Identifying and Treating Fever

Fever is generally recognized as an oral temperature above 99.5°F, a rectal temperature above 101°F, or an armpit temperature above 98.6°F. It is important to be aware of these benchmarks because the normal body temperature varies according to these different parts of the body. For example, 101°F does not always indicate a fever. This temperature is considered normal if taken rectally. However, if this same temperature is obtained orally, it does indicate a fever since normal oral temperature is 99.5°F.

Fever often accompanies a viral infection, bacterial infection, dehydration, body tissue damage (post-surgery), and chronic illness such as cancer or gout. If fever persists for more than three days, contact your physician.

The symptoms most often reported accompanying fever include sweating, headache, muscle pain, joint pain, back pain, rapid heart rate, flushing, exhaustion, and loss of appetite. The treatment of a fever is aimed at relieving these symptoms.

When treating a fever, all of the ingredients including aspirin, acetaminophen, ketoprofen, ibuprofen, and naproxen have about the same effectiveness when dosed appropriately. Often, acetaminophen is the preferred product due to the GI or stomach side effects that often occur with the use of aspirin, ketoprofen, ibuprofen, and naproxen.

Acetaminophen should be given to children who have flu-like symptoms or chickenpox due to the possibility of **Reye's Syndrome.**

A fever is usually a short-term, self-limiting symptom. If a fever is associated with back pain, abdominal pain, diarrhea, vomiting, stiff neck, painful urination, or seizure, contact your physician prior to treating.

Treating Pain or Fever

There are five ingredients that are available in non-prescription strengths to treat pain or fever: 1) aspirin, 2) acetaminophen, 3) ibuprofen, 4) ketoprofen, and 5) naproxen. The side effects associated with these medications vary greatly. If you have any illness or chronic condition that has been diagnosed, or is being treated with other medications, or if you are pregnant, it is important to consult your physician before taking any of these medications.

TABLE 2-1: Most Effective Analgesic and Anti-Pyretic Ingredients

Headache	Muscle Ache	Joint Pain	Swelling or Inflammation	Menstrual Pain	Fever
Aspirin	Aspirin	Aspirin	Aspirin	Aspirin	Aspirin
Acetamin-ophen	Ibuprofen	Acetamin-ophen*	Ibuprofen	Ibuprofen	Acetamino-phen
Ibuprofen	Ketoprofen	Ibuprofen	Ketoprofen	Ketoprofen	Ibuprofen
Ketoprofen	Naproxen	Ketoprofen	Naproxen	Naproxen	Ketoprofen
Naproxen		Naproxen			Naproxen

*Recent research is substantiating that acetaminophen can be effective in relieving the symptom of pain associated with osteoarthritis. It is currently considered the initial drug of choice for pain management. However, discuss this medication and others with your physician before self-treating either type of arthritis.

Note: Aspirin is effective for treating muscle pain, arthritis, or swelling, but often the dose is higher than is recommended for non-prescription use.

Combination Analgesic Products

Many OTC analgesic medications combine the primary ingredient with **caffeine** or an **antihistamine.**

For example, pain-relieving products that are indicated for use at bedtime are aimed at reducing pain while allowing you to get a good night's sleep. These products contain antihistamines and may cause drowsiness. Consider this if you must be mentally alert while taking the medication. These and other combination products reportedly increase the analgesic effect obtained with the medication. In addition, these products should be used with care in patients with **heart disease, high blood pressure** or other **long-term illness,** or in patients who currently take **other medications.**

It is important to remember that these products are often much more expensive than the single-ingredient products. This factor may play a role when choosing which product is best for you.

Analgesic and Anti-Fever Products

Table 2-2 (pages 50-52) lists the most commonly found OTC analgesic and anti-fever medications, their main ingredients, any other beneficial ingredients, and their dosage form(s). Several products contain the same active ingredients. Always read the product label for the amount of active ingredient contained per dose of medication.

Some medications have suggested dosages up to four tablets at a time while others require only one tablet to achieve the same result. Pay close attention to the dosing schedule. Some products are designed to be taken every 12 hours while others require dosing every four hours. This may be important to you if you do not have a schedule flexible enough to allow frequent dosing.

Summary

When choosing an analgesic or anti-pyretic medication, there are several factors that should be considered. Some brand-name products may have the exact same ingredients, but will have these ingredients in different amounts. For example, Tylenol™ Regular Strength and Extra Strength both contain acetaminophen. However, Tylenol™ Regular Strength contains 325mg, whereas Tylenol™ Extra Strength contains 500mg.

Other factors that should be considered include route of administration, dosage form, taste, dosing schedule, and price. Eckerd brand and generic forms of aspirin, acetaminophen, ibuprofen, and naproxen are available.

Ketoprofen is not yet available from generic manufacturers, and, is usually more expensive than either ibuprofen or naproxen generic products.

Always follow the directions on the package, and do not exceed the dosage. If pain persists for more than 10 days or fever persists for more than 3 days, contact your physician.

Thanks to the availability of OTC analgesic products, the symptoms associated with pain and fever are easy to treat.

When choosing the best product for you, consider your symptoms and if the ingredients found in each individual product are appropriate. After you decide which ingredient is best for you, consider dosage form (tablet, suppository, liquid), dosing schedule, and price.

If you are unsure which product is best for you, ask your Eckerd Pharmacist or physician for advice.

TABLE 2-2: Most Effective Analgesics or Anti-Pyretics for Treating Pain or Fever

National Brand Products	Eckerd Brand Products	Main Ingredient(s)	Added Ingredient(s)	Dosage Form(s)
Actron		Ketoprofen		Caplet
Advil	Ibuprofen	Ibuprofen		Caplet, Tablet
Aleve	Naproxen	Naproxen		Caplet, Tablet
Alka-Seltzer Extra Strength		Aspirin		Effervescent Tablet
Alka-Seltzer Original		Aspirin		Effervescent Tablet
Anacin	Adult Strength Aspirin	Aspirin	Caffeine	Tablet
Anacin Maximum Strength		Aspirin	Caffeine	Tablet
Ascriptin Arthritis Pain	Aspirin Plus Extra	Aspirin		Caplet
Ascriptin, Maximum and Regular		Aspirin		Caplet, Tablet
BC		Aspirin	Caffeine	Powder, Tablet
Backaid		Acetamin-ophen		Caplet
Bayer Aspirin (Original and Maximum)	Film Coated Aspirin (Regular and Maximum)	Aspirin		Caplet, Tablet
Bayer Children's Aspirin	Chewable Aspirin (Children's)	Aspirin		Chewable Tablet
Bayer Delayed Release Enteric Coated		Aspirin		Tablet, Caplet
Bayer Low Dose	Eckerd Low Dose	Aspirin		Tablet

continued

TABLE 2-2: Most Effective Analgesics or Anti-Pyretics for Treating Pain or Fever (continued)

National Brand Products	Eckerd Brand Products	Main Ingredient(s)	Added Ingredient(s)	Dosage Form(s)
Bufferin Extra Strength and Original	Buffered Aspirin	Aspirin		Caplet, Tablet
Doan's Extra Strength		Acetamin-ophen		Tablet
Ecotrin Adult Low Strength		Aspirin		Tablet
Ecotrin Maximum Strength and Regular	Eckerd Maximum Enteric	Aspirin		Tablet
Excedrin Aspirin Free		Acetamin-ophen	Caffeine	Caplet
Excedrin Extra Strength	Eckerd Super Strength	Aspirin, Acetamin-ophen	Caffeine	Caplet, Tablet
Feverall Junior Strength		Acetamin-ophen		Suppository
Goody's Extra Strength		Aspirin, Acetamin-ophen	Caffeine	Tablet
Midol Menstrual Max Strength Multi-Symptom		Acetamin-ophen	Caffeine	Caplet, Gelcap
Momemtum		Magnesium Salicylate		Caplet
Motrin, Children's		Ibuprofen		Suspension
Motrin IB	Ibuprofen	Ibuprofen		Caplet, Tablet, Gelcap
Nuprin	Ibuprofen	Ibuprofen		Tablet, Caplet
Orudis KT		Ketoprofen		Tablet

continued

TABLE 2-2: Most Effective Analgesics or Anti-Pyretics for Treating Pain or Fever (continued)

National Brand Products	Eckerd Brand Products	Main Ingredient(s)	Added Ingredient(s)	Dosage Form(s)
Percogesic Coated		Acetamin-ophen	Phenyltolox-amine (Antihista-mine)	Tablet
Tempra (1, 2, & 3)		Acetamin-ophen		Drops, Syrup, Chewable Tablet
Tylenol Extended Relief		Acetamin-ophen		Time-released Tablet
Tylenol Extra Strength	Extra Strength Non-Aspirin Pain Relief	Acetamin-ophen		Geltab, Caplet
Tylenol Extra Strength Adult Pain Reliever		Acetamin-ophen		Liquid
Tylenol Junior Strength	Eckerd Junior Strength	Acetamin-ophen		Chewable Tablet, Caplet
Tylenol Regular Strength		Acetamin-ophen		Caplet, Tablet, Gelcap
Tylenol Children's	Children's Non-Aspirin Fever and Pain Reliever	Acetamin-ophen		Elixir, Chewable Tablet, Suspension
Tylenol Infant's	Infant's Non-Aspirin Pain Relief	Acetamin-open		Drops
Vanquish		Aspirin, Acetamin-ophen	Caffeine	Caplet

Notes Pertaining to Your Personal OTC Drug Preferences

_____

_____

_____

_____

_____

_____

_____

_____

_____

_____

_____

_____

_____

_____

_____

_____

_____

_____

_____

_____

_____

_____

_____

_____

_____

It's right at Eckerd!

A First-Aid Checklist

Your home is the first step for first-aid treatment. So, when a problem occurs, you want to be ready to respond. Our Eckerd Pharmacists have created this helpful first-aid checklist, those critical first-aid items your home and family should not be without.

- ☐ Aspirin
- ☐ Ibuprofen
- ☐ Ipecac syrup
- ☐ Peroxide
- ☐ Alcohol prep pads
- ☐ Antibiotic ointment
- ☐ Calamine lotion
- ☐ Hydrocortisone cream
- ☐ Anti-fungal cream

- ☐ Bandage scissors
- ☐ Tweezers
- ☐ Regular scissors
- ☐ Knife
- ☐ Latex gloves
- ☐ Safety pins
- ☐ SAM™ splint
- ☐ Ice bag
- ☐ Thermometer
- ☐ Adhesive strip bandages (various sizes)

- ☐ Trauma dressings
- ☐ Eye patches
- ☐ Tape
- ☐ Insect repellent
- ☐ Acetaminophen (for pain)
- ☐ Instant ice pack
- ☐ Non-stick pads
- ☐ Antiseptic towelettes
- ☐ Cotton-tipped swabs

Get updates to the information in this book at the **Eckerd Corporation Home Page** on the World Wide Web. Visit us often at **www.eckerd.com.**

Chapter Three

Choosing the Proper Antacid/Anti-Ulcer Product

3

Antacids are used either to **neutralize** stomach acid or to **prevent** the production of excess acids in the gastrointestinal (GI) tract. This change in acidity creates an increase in the **pH** of the stomach and provides short-term relief of **indigestion** and **heartburn,** and long-term relief of specific GI diseases.

The antacids that were first available without prescription are intended to neutralize acid that is already present in the stomach. These types of antacids are referred to as **non-H2-Antagonists.**

Recently, a new class of over-the-counter drugs has been introduced that was once available only by a physician's prescription. These drugs, known as **H2-Antagonists,** prevent the production of gastric acid by the stomach instead of neutralizing the acid that is already present.

Symptoms of gastrointestinal disorders can often be quite severe and may include any of the following:

- Burning sensation in the upper stomach or chest
- Feeling of nausea
- Abdominal or stomach pain (may or may not be relieved with food)

Antacids (non-H2-Antagonists and H2-Antagonists) are recommended for the following uses:

1) excessive acid or heartburn,
2) acid indigestion,
3) stomach upset, and
4) gastrointestinal diseases, which may include gastroesophageal reflux disease (GERD), peptic ulcer, gastric ulcer, and duodenal ulcer diseases.

Physiology

The stomach has three main responsibilities: 1) the storing of food, 2) the mixing of food with gastric or stomach secretions, and 3) the emptying of food into the small intestine for its proper digestion and absorption by the small intestine.

Gastric acid aids in the digestion and absorption of food as well as in the maintenance of a stable environment by killing bacteria found in the stomach. Having a proper balance of acid is important. When an excessive amount of acid is present, GI problems may occur.

The primary cell of the body involved in hydrochloric acid secretion in the stomach is the **parietal** cell. The pH of the stomach acid is approximately 0.8—which is extremely acidic—and is about three million times more acidic than the pH of the blood in our arteries.

The stomach is protected by a lining that is called the **mucosal** lining. This lining is made of cells that secrete mucus and **bicarbonate** which helps create a barrier of protection.

Factors that can disrupt this mucosal lining and, thus, lead to stomach problems include: other medications (both prescription or non-prescription), alcohol, smoking, caffeine, certain diseases, and an organism called *Helicobacter pylori*. When acid levels become too high, heartburn, gas, reflux, "upset stomach," indigestion, or more seriously, ulcers can result.

Fortunately, there are many medications that can aid in short-term and even long-term relief. However, if problems still persist or are not relieved after two weeks, a physician should be consulted to rule out other possibilities. If bleeding is apparent in vomit, urine, or feces, do not self-medicate. Consult your physician immediately. A more serious condition may be present.

Lifestyle Changes CAN Make a Difference!

For many years it was believed that a diet of spicy or acidic foods would increase symptoms of GI disease. Studies have shown that special, **bland diets** have no benefit. However, foods that should be avoided are caffeinated beverages, foods that contain caffeine (including chocolate), and alcohol. Also, avoid peppermint and acidic juices such as orange or tomato because they have been associated with causing increased acid production.

It is important to remember that many prescription and OTC medications also contain caffeine and/or alcohol. These ingredients are found on the OTC product labels. Ask your Eckerd Pharmacist if your prescription medications contain caffeine or alcohol.

Acid production increases after food intake. Therefore, it is best to eat three meals every day and to refrain from snacking at bedtime. If you have a late night snack, more acid will be produced while you sleep. This acid production can make your symptoms much worse.

Treatment of Gastrointestinal and Stomach Disorders

Antacids—**non-H2-Antagonists**—help to **neutralize** the gastric acid secreted by the parietal cells. These antacids do not affect the amount or rate of acid that is secreted. They only neutralize the acid that is already present. This improves the ability of the mucosal lining to act as a defense barrier.

Conversely, the **H2-Antagonists** exert their action by **blocking** the formation of hydrochloric acid in the stomach. Currently, four H2-Antagonists are available in non-prescription strengths. In general, all four are equally effective when taken appropriately. It is important to remember that the H2-Antagonists block the formation of acid and, therefore, take longer to give relief if an abundance of acid is already present.

For chronic conditions such as a **hyperacidic** stomach or **duodenal ulcers,** their ability to block acid formation is the key to their success.

We will discuss the two types of antacids separately in this chapter, as they differ in the way they work in the body.

Antacids (Non-H2-Antagonists)

All antacid products, excluding the H2-antagonist type, contain at least one of the following ingredients: calcium carbonate, sodium bicarbonate, aluminum salts, or magnesium salts. These ingredients differ in potency, side effects, and interactions with other medications and the body itself. It is important to identify which ingredient is best to treat your symptom(s).

Other considerations that are very important when you choose an antacid medication include the taste of the product, dosage form (tablet, suspension, gum, lozenge, etc.), dosing schedule (with or without food), and cost. Some antacids have added other ingredients such as **simethicone** which treats gas (flatulence).

Antacids Containing Calcium Carbonate

Antacids containing **calcium carbonate** are very potent and neutralize acids well. These antacids are intended for short-term use only and should not be used for long-term therapy. In comparison to other antacids, they take longer to dissolve, but ultimately neutralize the acid to a greater degree.

Many people now assume that antacids containing calcium carbonate are a good source of dietary calcium. Such a small percent of the calcium is actually absorbed that this is simply not true.

Antacids Containing Sodium Bicarbonate

Antacids containing sodium bicarbonate are potent and give almost **immediate relief.** These antacids are intended for short-term therapy only and should not be taken for long periods of time. Care should be taken if you have 1) a **sodium or salt-restricted diet,** 2) **congestive heart failure,** 3) **high blood pressure,** 4) **cirrhosis,** 5) **edema (swelling),** or 6) **renal (kidney) failure or insufficiency.** Some of the sodium contained in these antacids is absorbed by the body and can add to your problems.

When choosing which antacid is best for you always read the "other" ingredients on the package. Some products contain aspirin or acetaminophen (Tylenol™) as well. The amount of aspirin found in some antacids can actually cause stomach upset or ulceration.

Antacids Containing Aluminum Salts

Antacids containing **aluminum salts** dissolve very slowly in the stomach, but often take longer to work than other antacids. Salt forms of the antacids are found in three types: 1) **hydroxide,** 2) **carbonate,** and 3) **phosphate.** The hydroxide salt is the most common form used as an antacid. However, when compared to other types of antacids, the aluminum hydroxide antacids simply do not neutralize stomach acid as well.

Constipation is the most common complaint associated with aluminum salt antacids. This is important to remember if you have bowel problems or are often constipated. Many aluminum salt antacids are combined with magnesium salts to prevent the constipation which sometimes occurs.

People with **renal** failure or renal insufficiency should not use aluminum salt antacids due to the possible risk of absorption of the aluminum. Elevated aluminum concentrations in the body can cause very serious problems.

Antacids Containing Magnesium Salts

Antacids that contain **magnesium salts** are potent, but do not provide long-term relief. They neutralize acid better than the aluminum salt antacids, but not as well as the calcium carbonate or sodium bicarbonate type antacids.

Diarrhea is the most common side effect associated with their use. Therefore, if you have chronic diarrhea due to such illnesses as **colitis** or **Crohn's disease,** this type of antacid is not suitable for your needs. For this reason, some antacids combine aluminum salts with magnesium salts to avoid this unwanted side effect.

People with **renal** failure or renal insufficiency should not use magnesium salt antacids. Excessive levels of magnesium in the body have been associated with life-threatening problems.

Antacids Containing Combination Products

Many antacids are formulated by combining several different ingredients. The most common combination consists of magnesium and aluminum which are combined to eliminate the side effects associated when magnesium and aluminum are taken alone.

Another combination is one of **sodium bicarbonate** combined with **alginic acid**. Although, alginic acid is not an antacid, in the presence of saliva, it reacts with sodium bicarbonate to make a "foam" that effectively relieves heartburn. Other combinations are shown in Table 3-5 (page 63).

Simethicone Containing Products

Some products contain only simethicone. Simethicone is an **anti-gas** product. The OTC products that only contain simethicone are shown in Table 3-6 (page 64). Products that **only** contain simethicone will **only** relieve gas. If you have symptoms in addition to gas, then a combination product containing an antacid in combination with simethicone will be a better choice.

A combination product will usually be less expensive than buying both an antacid along with another product that contains simethicone separately.

H2-Antagonist OTC Medications

The **H2-Antagonist** medications only recently became available without prescription. These were originally marketed for peptic ulcer diseases (gastric ulcer, peptic ulcer), as well as other GI diseases, but are now marketed at OTC doses for heartburn, acid relief, and "sour" stomach.

H2-Antagonists very effectively *block the formation of acid* in the stomach. However, H2-Antagonists are not effective in *neutralizing the acid that is already present.* When taken appropriately, all of the H2-Antagonist OTC medications are effective for treating GI symptoms.

Take these medications only as directed on the package. Do not take the maximum daily dosage for more than two weeks unless under the advice and supervision of a physician. If your symptoms do not subside in two weeks, consult your Eckerd Pharmacist or physician for advice.

Points to Remember

Self-treatment of GI disorders such as heartburn, "upset stomach", indigestion, gas, reflux, ulcers, etc., can prove to be quite effective. There are many considerations to take into account when choosing which OTC antacid/anti-ulcer medication is the best for you. Read the label on the bottle to look for sodium content, sugar content, and so on. Also, take into account the dosage form (tablet, suspension, gum, lozenge, etc.), dosing schedule (with or without food), taste, and cost. Liquid forms of antacids are absorbed faster and, therefore, give faster relief than do other dosage forms. If you are taking a chewable tablet, be certain to chew it thoroughly and drink a large glass of water afterwards. This will assure the best results.

Before taking any medication, always read the warning label on the container to make sure the medication will not interfere with any other medications that you may take or other diseases that you may have. Some drugs actually bind to the antacid and are not absorbed to their full extent. If you are presently taking a prescription medication, consult your Eckerd pharmacist or physician before taking an OTC antacid or anti-ulcer medication.

Bleeding is a serious complication that occurs with some ulcers. As many as 20% of people with ulcers experience bleeding. If you have symptoms that suggest bleeding such as black tarry stools or the appearance of "coffee grounds" in your vomit, **consult your physician immediately. Do not self treat!**

If you are pregnant, consult your physician before taking any OTC medication including antacid medications.

Antacids are very effective in relieving symptoms associated with 1) excessive acid (heartburn), 2) acid indigestion, 3) stomach upset, and 4) gastrointestinal diseases which may include gastroesophageal reflux disease (GERD), peptic ulcer, gastric ulcer, and duodenal ulcer diseases. However, certain GI diseases are best treated with medications that are available only by prescription. If your doctor has already prescribed a medication for you, do not discontinue its use or start self-medicating with an OTC antacid product without first consulting with him.

Remember, antacids should not be used for more than two weeks. If symptoms are still present after this time, contact your physician.

Table 3-1: Antacids Containing Calcium Carbonate

National Brand Products	Eckerd Brand Products	Dosage Form(s)	Simethicone Added?
Children's Mylanta Upset Stomach Relief		Chewable Tablet, Liquid	
Chooz		Gum	
Rolaids Sodium Free		Chewable Tablet	
Rolaids Calcium Rich	Calcium Rich Antacid Tablets	Chewable Tablet	Yes
Rolaids Extra Strength		Chewable Tablet	Yes
Titralac (Regular & Extra Strength)		Chewable Tablet	
Titralac Plus		Chewable Tablet, Liquid	Yes
Tums (Regular & Extra Strength)	Antacid Tablets (Regular & Ex/Strength)	Chewable Tablet	
Tums Ultra	Ultra Antacid	Chewable Tablet	
Tums Anti-Gas/Antacid		Chewable Tablet	Yes

TABLE 3-2: Antacids Containing Sodium Bicarbonate

National Brand Products	Eckerd Brand Products	Dosage Form(s)	Other
Alka-Seltzer (Flavored, Extra Strength, Original)	Effervescent Pain Relief	Effervescent Tablets	Aspirin
Alka-Seltzer Gold		Effervescent Tablets	
Brioschi		Effervescent Tablet	
Bromo-Seltzer		Effervescent (granular)	Acetaminophen

TABLE 3-3: Antacids Containing Aluminum Salts

Generic Name	Eckerd Brand Products	Dosage Form(s)
Alternagel	Hydroxide	Liquid

TABLE 3-4: Antacids Containing Magnesium Salts

National Brand Products	Eckerd Brand Products	Dosage Form(s)
Phillips Milk of Magnesia	Milk of Magnesia	Chewable Tablet, Suspension

TABLE 3-5: Combination Antacid Products

National Brand Products	Eckerd Brand Products	Main Ingredients	Dosage Form(s)	Other
Di-Gel		Calcium Carbonate, Magnesium Hydroxide	Chewable Tablet, Liquid	Simeth-icone
Gaviscon, Gaviscon-2	Antacid Chewable Tabs	Aluminum Hydroxide, Magnesium Trisilicate, Sodium Bicarbonate	Chewable Tablet	Alginic Acid
Gaviscon ESR, Gaviscon ESRF		Aluminum Hydroxide, Magnesium Carbonate	Chewable Tablet, Suspension	Alginic Acid (ESR)
Gelusil		Aluminum Hydroxide, Magnesium Hydroxide	Tablet	Simeth-icone
Maalox	Antacid Suspension	Aluminum Hydroxide, Magnesium Hydroxide	Suspension	
Maalox	Antacid Tablets	Aluminum Hydroxide, Magnesium Hydroxide	Tablet	
Maalox Antacid plus Anti-Gas	Antacid Plus	Aluminum Hydroxide, Magnesium Hydroxide	Tablet	Simeth-icone
Maalox Extra Strength Plus	Extra Strength Antacid Plus	Aluminum Hydroxide, Magnesium Hydroxide	Suspension	Simeth-icone
Mylanta (Regular & Double Strength)	Antacid with Simethicone, Antacid with Simethicone II	Aluminum Hydroxide, Magnesium Hydroxide	Gelcap, Chewable Tablet, Suspension	Simeth-icone
Rolaids Calcium & Magnesium		Calcium Carbonate, Magnesium Hydroxide	Tablet	

◀ 63

TABLE 3-6: Simethicone-Containing OTC Products

National Brand Products	Eckerd Brand Products	Dosage Form(s)
Gas-X (Regular & Extra Strength)	Gas Relief Tablets	Chewable Tablet
Maalox Anti-Gas	Gas Relief Tablets	Tablet
Maalox Extra Strength Anti-Gas		Tablet
Mylanta Gas	Gas Relief Tabs	Tablet
Mylicon Infant's Drops	Anti-Gas Drops	Drops

TABLE 3-7: H2-Antagonist OTC Medications

National Brand Products	Dosage Form(s)
Tagamet HB	Tablet
Zantac 75	Tablet
Axid AR	Tablet
Pepcid AC	Tablet
Mylanta AR	Tablet

Notes Pertaining to Your Personal OTC Drug Preferences

_____

_____

_____

_____

_____

_____

_____

_____

_____

_____

_____

_____

_____

_____

_____

_____

_____

_____

_____

_____

It's right at Eckerd!

Your Eckerd Pharmacist Has the Answer

With each new prescription your doctor orders for you, you receive a <u>free</u> **Eckerd Rx Advisor** instruction summary. This comprehensive summary gives you the important information you need regarding dosages, side effects, cautions, your doctor's special instructions, and other pertinent information.

Always make sure you have all the answers you need. If for any reason you are not perfectly clear about an instruction from your doctor or from us, *ask!* And always feel free to ask these important questions of your Eckerd Pharmacist:

1. What is the name of the medicine? What is it supposed to do?
2. How much of the medicine should I take, when should I take it, and for how long?
3. What foods, beverages, other medicines, or activities should I avoid while taking this new medication?
4. What are the possible side effects and what should I do if they occur?
5. Can I obtain a generic or a less expensive brand of this medication?
6. Will this new prescription work safely with the other prescription and nonprescription medicines I am currently taking?
7. May I obtain refills?

The Eckerd Rx Advisor is now also available in Spanish and in large-type formats. Ask your pharmacist.

Get updates to the information in this book at the **Eckerd Corporation Home Page** on the World Wide Web. Visit us often at **www.eckerd.com.**

Chapter Four

Choosing the Proper Anti-Diarrheal or Laxative Product

4

Body Function

The small intestine is responsible for maintaining normal bowel function by aiding in digestion, absorbing nutrients, and retaining waste materials.

In the small intestine, food is reduced to a substance that consists of undigested food particles, nutrients, water, electrolytes, and bacteria. This substance passes to the colon where it is stored until defecation occurs. If the proper balance between the absorption and secretion of fluids is not maintained, diarrhea or constipation will occur.

Causes and Symptoms of Diarrhea

Diarrhea is defined as the acute or chronic, and frequent amount of fecal matter lost from the bowel. The many factors that lead to diarrhea are: bacterial infections, viral infections, protozoal infections, food intolerance, disease (for example, Crohn's, colitis, AIDS), or alcohol allergies or poisonings.

Mild, uncomplicated diarrhea generally only lasts for a couple of days, but it may be quite bothersome and, therefore, may require treatment for the symptoms. Anti-diarrheal products should be used **only for temporary, short-term relief.**

Note: If symptoms of diarrhea persist for more than two days, are accompanied by a high fever, cause greater than 5% total body weight loss, or involve stools that are bloody, contact your physician immediately.

When diarrhea occurs, an excessive amount of fluid and electrolyte loss can occur, leading to dehydration. The symptoms of dehydration may include dry mouth, sunken eyes, weakness, low urinary output, and dizziness. **Fluid replacement** is very important when diarrhea is present. This can be accomplished by drinking clear fluids and/or sugar-electrolyte formulations such as Gatorade or products that can also be found in your Eckerd Pharmacy, such as Eckerd Brand Pediatric Electrolyte™, Kao Electrolyte™, or Pedialyte™.

Hydration should be taken very seriously. If diarrhea symptoms are severe and dehydration occurs, it may be necessary to replace fluids intravenously.

Other non-medical measures may facilitate the disappearance of symptoms. These measures include rest, proper diet, and the avoidance of dairy products.

Medications Used to Treat Diarrhea

The most commonly used non-prescription anti-diarrheal medication currently available is **loperamide.** It is the drug of choice for treating uncomplicated diarrhea. It not only reduces the frequency of stool loss, but also helps relieve the cramping that often accompanies diarrhea.

Loperamide is also effective in treating **Traveler's Diarrhea**. Traveler's Diarrhea is caused by eating or drinking fecally-contaminated food or water that is not inactivated by cooking or processing. Typically, symptoms occur within 24 to 48 hours of exposure and include diarrhea, nausea, fever, chills, and muscle pain. Table 4-1 on page 74 shows the current products which are available at your Eckerd Pharmacy.

Note: Loperamide should not be used for more than two days for acute diarrhea.

Many anti-diarrheal products contain **adsorbents** that both help to alleviate the symptoms such as gastric pain, that accompany diarrhea, and also absorb the excessive fluid that is present with diarrhea.

Often large quantities of adsorbents are necessary to accomplish an anti-diarrheal effect. Constipation may result if adsorbents are taken in excess. Table 4-2 (page 74) shows the current products that contain adsorbents which are available at your Eckerd Pharmacy.

The other OTC anti-diarrheal products available contain **bismuth subsalicylate.** These products can be used to control diarrhea, relieve abdominal cramping and stop Traveler's Diarrhea. Brand-name products include Pepto-Bismol Maximum Strength™, Pepto-Bismol Regular Strength™, and various generic products.

Because these products contain aspirin or other salicylates, they should be used with caution if you have renal problems, currently take aspirin products, have a bleeding disorder, or are allergic to aspirin.

Constipation may result with the excessive use of these products and, therefore, they should be used only for short-term relief. A black tarry stool is often associated with the use of bismuth subsalicylate. This tarry appearance does not necessarily indicate blood in the stool.

Summary

Anti-diarrheal products are quite effective in relieving the bothersome symptoms caused by diarrhea. Like all medications, these products should be used with caution if you are taking any other OTC or prescription medications. Pregnant or nursing mothers should consult their Eckerd Pharmacist or physician before taking these products.

Anti-diarrheal products should be used for **temporary short-term relief only.** If symptoms of diarrhea persist for more than two days, are accompanied by a high fever, cause greater than 5% total body weight loss, or if stools are bloody, contact your physician immediately.

Causes and Symptoms of Constipation

Constipation is defined as the decrease in bowel movement for an individual based on what is "normal" for that individual. Constipation may be caused by not drinking enough water or other fluids, not having enough fiber in the diet, improper dietary intake, not acting on the need to defecate, or lack of exercise. Symptoms often include lower back pain, stomach distention, and headache.

Unfortunately, **laxatives are often abused**—most often to promote weight loss. The excessive use of laxatives is very dangerous and can lead to severe problems such as vitamin and mineral loss, and dependence on the laxative. Laxatives should only be used for short-term therapy—not more than one week—and should be discontinued when bowel movement regularity returns. If constipation is accompanied by nausea, vomiting, rectal bleeding, dizziness, or weakness, consult your physician before self-medicating.

Constipation can often be relieved without taking a laxative product. However, if symptoms are bothersome and a laxative is chosen, several factors should be considered. Laxatives vary greatly in their onset of action, site of action (colon, small intestine, large intestine), dosage form, dosing frequency, taste, side effects, and price.

There are six main classifications of laxatives: 1) bulk-forming, 2) stimulants, 3) surfactants, 4) lubricants, 5) saline, and 6) miscellaneous. It is very important that you understand how these products differ and how you can use them for your specific need.

Many laxatives cause discoloration of the feces or urine. Always read the warning label on the product before taking any medication.

Bulk-Forming Laxatives

Bulk-forming laxatives cause water to be retained in the small and large intestines. This water helps to produce formed stools. Bulk-forming laxatives are the best choice for the initial treatment of constipation. They are made from natural sources such as plants or vegetables, most of which are not absorbed by the body. They produce bulk in the form of a gel that passes easily through the intestines.

Bulk-forming laxatives generally take 12 to 24 hours to work, but they can take as long as 72 hours. It is very important that you drink a large glass of water (8 ounces) when taking these laxatives. Not only does the water promote stool formation, but it also prevents obstruction from occurring in the intestines or, if you have difficulty swallowing, in the throat area.

Several of these bulk-forming preparations are indicated as grit free. These products mask the gritty texture that is associated with many of the powdered bulk laxatives. Also, there are some products that are labeled as "sugar free." These products are ideal for diabetics.

Bulk-forming laxatives are the safest form of laxatives for long-term use. If you have diet restrictions such limited carbohydrate intake, consult your physician before choosing these products.

When choosing which bulk-forming laxative is right for you, consider the dosage form, flavor (orange, original, lemon-lime, etc.), price, and dosing schedule.

The main ingredients in bulk-forming laxatives are methylcellulose, polycarbophil, tragacanth, and psyllium. Table 4-3 (page 75) shows bulk-forming laxatives and their dosage form(s).

Stimulant Laxatives

Stimulant laxatives are most commonly used to empty the colon prior to rectal and bowel examinations, as well as for use in surgical procedures involving the gastrointestinal tract. They **should never be used routinely.**

These laxatives stimulate the secretion of fluids by the intestines. Their effectiveness depends on the dosage given. Because they react fairly quickly, they are often abused. Abuse can lead to dehydration, loss of protein, loss of potassium, severe cramping, or a dysfunctional colon.

Because these products do have a quick onset of action, it is best **not** to use them at certain times (for example, at bedtime).

When used with **extreme caution** or under the advice of a physician, however, stimulant laxatives can be very effective. Laxatives containing cascara sagrada or senna should be used with caution in nursing mothers. Cascara sagrada is excreted in the breast milk and can cause diarrhea in the nursing infant. Table 4-4 (page 76) shows the OTC stimulant laxatives, their ingredients, onset of action, and dosage form(s).

Surfactant Laxatives

Laxatives that contain only **surfactants** should *not* be used to relieve long-term constipation. These laxatives are considered "stool softeners." They work best to *prevent* rather than cure constipation. These laxatives are best for people who should not strain while having a bowel movement such as new mothers, post-rectal or vaginal surgery patients, and persons with heart disease or high blood pressure.

Many of these products contain **sodium.** If you have a condition such as high **blood pressure, take other medications, or are on a low-sodium diet,** consult your physician before taking this medication.

When taking a stool softener, it is important that you remember to drink a lot of water. This will help the medication work faster and more effectively. Be patient! These medications generally take up to two days to work. However, they can take as long as five days. They are intended for short-term use only to soften stools that are too hard to pass. Long-term use should only be considered if recommended by your physician.

Table 4-5 (page 77) shows the laxative products that contain stool softeners, their dosage form(s), and ingredients.

Lubricant Laxatives

Mineral oil is sometimes used to help with constipation in cases where straining during defecation should be avoided. Mineral oil coats and softens the stool, thus allowing for easy passage. Mineral oil enemas are often used to break up fecal impaction.

Use mineral oil **only at the direction of a physician.** There is a chance that mineral oil can cause anal itching, hemorrhoids, or other severe conditions. Liquid forms of mineral oil can be aspirated into the lungs and cause lipid pneumonia. Mineral oil can decrease the absorption of vitamins A, D, E, and K and may decrease the amount of vitamin K that is available to the fetus in pregnant women.

If mineral oil is recommended by your physician, use products that have been **emulsified** to help improve the flavor of the product. There is evidence that these emulsified products may also soften fecal matter more effectively than the unemulsified products. When required, take mineral oil on an empty stomach.

Saline Laxatives

Saline laxatives are derived from salt forms of magnesium or sodium and help to draw water into the stool. They are used to rid the colon of wastes for rectal and bowel examinations or prior to surgery, and to rid the body of drugs in cases of possible poisonings. These laxatives should not be taken for simple constipation.

Magnesium citrate is ordered very commonly by physicians when a rectal exam is to be done. This medication is much better if refrigerated prior to drinking.

Due to some absorption of the drug, caution must be given in patients with renal impairment if a magnesium laxative is given, or for people who should avoid sodium if a sodium-based laxative is given.

Other Types of Laxatives

Glycerin is usually administered in the form of an enema or suppository and is generally quite safe and generally effective within 15 to 30 minutes. Both infant and adult suppositories are available. Consult with your physician or Eckerd Pharmacist before administering glycerin suppositories to an infant.

Combination Products

Some laxatives are available as combinations of more than one type of laxative. For example, some bulk-forming laxative products are combined with stimulant laxatives. The stimulant laxative is added to increase the onset of action. Other combinations may include stimulant laxative products combined with stool softeners.

These products must be used with **extreme care.** While one ingredient may be safe and effective for you, the other ingredient may not. If you are unsure about which product is best for you, consult your pharmacist or physician. Table 4-9 (page 79) shows the OTC combination laxative products.

Summary

There are many anti-diarrheal and laxative products currently available. These products should only be used for a short-term basis unless otherwise instructed by your physician. When choosing which product is best for you, consider the onset of action, dosage form, dosing frequency, side effects, and price. Always read the warnings on the product label and follow the directions carefully. If you need help in deciding which medication is best for you, consult your Eckerd Pharmacist or physician.

TABLE 4-1: OTC Anti-Diarrheal Products That Contain Loperamide

National Brand Products	Eckerd Brand Products	Dosage Form(s)
Diar Aid		Caplet
Imodium A-D	Anti-Diarrheal Liquid	Liquid
Imodium A-D	Anti-Diarrheal Caplets	Caplet
Kaopectate 1-D		Caplet
Maalox Anti-Diarrheal		Caplet
Pepto Diarrhea Control	Anti-Diarrheal Liquid	Liquid

TABLE 4-2: OTC Anti-Diarrheal Products That Contain Adsorbents

National Brand Products	Dosage Form(s)
Charco-Caps	Caplet, Capsule, Tablet
Diasorb	Liquid, Tablet
Donnagel	Chewable Tablet, Suspension
Kaopectate	Liquid
Kaopectate Children s	Chewable Tablet, Liquid
Parapectolin	Suspension
Rheaban	Caplet

TABLE 4-3: OTC Bulk-Forming Laxatives

National Brand Products	Eckerd Brand Products	Active Ingredient	Dosage Form(s)
Citrucel (Regular and Sugar Free)		Methylcellulose	Powder
Equalactin		Polycarbophil	Chewable Tablet
Fibercon	Fiber Tablets	Polycarbophil	Tablet
Fiberall		Polycarbophil	Tablet
Fiberall (Oatmeal Raisin)		Psyllium	Wafer
Fiberall (Orange)		Psyllium	Powder
Konsyl		Psyllium	Powder
Konsyl Fiber		Polycarbophil	Tablet
Metamucil Fiber (Apple Crisp)		Psyllium	Wafer
Metamucil (Original and Sugar Free)		Psyllium	Packet
Metamucil (Original Texture)	Natural Fiber Powder	Psyllium	Powder
Metamucil (Smooth Texture-Orange, Regular)	Smooth Natural Fiber Powder (Citrus, Orange)	Psyllium	Powder
Metamucil (Smooth Texture-Sugar Free, Citrus)	Smooth Natural Fiber Powder S/F (Citrus, Orange)	Psyllium	Powder
Perdiem Fiber		Psyllium	Granule

TABLE 4-4: OTC Stimulant Laxatives

National Brand Products	Eckerd Brand Products	Stimulant Ingredients	Onset of Action	Dosage Form(s)
Alophen		Phenoph-thalein	6–10 hours	Tablet
Dulcolax	Bisacodyl Laxative (Suppository, Tabs)	Bisacodyl	Oral: 6–10 hours Rectal: 15–60 min.	Suppository, Tablet
Evac-U-Gen		Phenoph-thalein	6–10 hours	Chewable Tablet
Ex-Lax Chocolate	Chocolate-Flavored Laxative Tabs	Phenoph-thalein	6–10 hours	Tablet
Ex-Lax Gentle Nature		Sennosides	8–12 hours	Tablet
Ex-Lax (Regular or Maximum)		Phenoph-thalein	6–10 hours	Tablet
Fleet		Bisacodyl	15–60 min.	Suppository, Tablet, Enema
Fletcher's Castoria		Senna	8–12 hours	Liquid
Fletcher's Children's Cherry		Phenolph-thalein	6–10 hours	Liquid
Kellogg's Tasteless Castor Oil	Castor Oil	Castor Oil	2–6 hours	Liquid
Milk of Magnesia Cascara		Cascara Sagrada	8–12 hours	Suspension
Modane		Phenolph-thalein	6–10 hours	Tablet
Nature's Remedy		Cascara Sagrada, Aloe	8–12 hours	Tablet
Senokot	Senna-C	Senna	8–12 hours	Tablet

TABLE 4-5: OTC Products
Containing Surfactant Laxatives

National Brand Products	Eckerd Brand Products	Generic Product	Dosage Form(s)
Colace	Docusate Sodium	Docusate Sodium	Capsule, Liquid, Syrup
Correctol Stool Softener Laxative		Docusate Sodium	Softgel
Ex-lax Stool Softener		Docusate Sodium	Caplet
Surfak		Docusate Calcium	Liqui-gel

TABLE 4-6: OTC Laxatives
Containing Mineral Oil

National Brand Products	Eckerd Brand Products	Dosage Form(s)
Fleet Mineral Oil Enema		Enema
Haley's M-O (Regular or Flavored)		Emulsion
Squibb's Mineral Oil (Oral)	Mineral Oil	Emulsion

TABLE 4-7: OTC Saline Laxatives

National Brand Products	Eckerd Brand Products	Saline Ingredient	Dosage Form(s)
Epsom Salt	Epsom Salt	Magnesium Sulfate	Granule
Fleet Ready to Use Enema		Sodium Phosphate	Enema
Fleet Ready to Use Enema for Children		Sodium Phosphate	Enema
Nature's Remedy		Sodium Biphosphate Sodium Phosphate	Enema
Phillips Milk of Magnesia	Milk of Magnesia (Regular or Flavored)	Magnesium Hydroxide	Chewable Tablet, Suspension

TABLE 4-8: OTC Glycerin Laxatives

National Brand Products	Eckerd Brand Products	Dosage Form(s)
Fleet Babylax	Glycerin Suppository Infant size	Liquid
Fleet Glycerin (Adult & Children)	Glycerin Suppository (Adult & Children)	Suppository
Fleet Glycerin Rectal Applicators		Liquid
Fleet Maximum-Strength Glycerin		Suppository

TABLE 4-9: OTC Combination Laxative Products

National Brand Products	Eckerd Brand Products	Active Ingredients	Dosage Form(s)
Correctol	Gentle Laxative	Stimulant: Phenophthalein Stool Softener: Docusate Sodium	Caplet, Tablet
Doxidan	Laxative plus Stool Softener	Stimulant: Phenophthalein Stool Softener: Docusate Sodium	Liqui-gel
Ex-Lax Extra Gentle		Stimulant: Phenophthalein Stool Softener: Docusate Sodium	Tablet
Feen-A-Mint Pills		Stimulant: Phenophthalein Stool Softener: Docusate Sodium	Tablet
Perdiem		Bulk-Former: Psyllium Stimulant: Senna	Granule
Peri-Colace	Casanthranol and Docusate Sodium	Stimulant: Casanthranol Stool Softener: Docusate Sodium	Tablet
Senokot-S		Stimulant: Senna Stool Softener: Docusate Sodium	Tablet

It's right at Eckerd!

New Ideas. Low Prices.

Your Eckerd Store is dedicated to helping you save money. Every week over 250 products are on sale, proving that you can look to, and count on, Eckerd for savings on the products you use most.

We always honor any of our competitor's advertised prices and we accept their coupons on everything in our store—including prescriptions. In fact, when it comes to prescription prices, we won't be beat. If you find a lower price anywhere—*including AARP or any local competitor*—just let us know. We'll match it. <u>Guaranteed</u>!

You can count on Eckerd to have the latest in over-the-counter medications, too, and quality, money-saving Eckerd brand products and medications.

Your Eckerd Pharmacy is filled with new and helpful products and ideas for healthful, happy living, plus ways to help you save time and money. We invite you to make Eckerd a part of your weekly shopping routine.

Get updates to the information in this book at the **Eckerd Corporation Home Page** on the World Wide Web. Visit us often at **www.eckerd.com**.

Chapter Five

Choosing the Proper Sleep-Aid or Stimulant Product

Most Americans claim they need eight hours of sleep or more per night. This number actually varies from one person to another, and from day to day. There is no "normal" amount of sleep that is required for the population as a whole. Sleep requirements vary greatly, depending on the individual. One person may need only five to six hours of sleep in one night to feel totally rested and alert the next day, whereas another person may need nine to ten hours of sleep to feel the same way.

Many products that affect the sleep pattern are currently available over-the-counter (OTC). **Sleep-aid products** are available to help improve the sleep pattern. **Stimulants** (caffeine-containing products) are also available for those who need to "stay awake" for various reasons.

Stages of Sleep

There are four main stages of sleep. Our body responds differently to each stage. Stages three and four are known as "deep sleep" stages. Stages three and four are not as lengthy in the elderly population and, therefore, elderly persons may require "cat naps" during the day and may also complain more of the inability to sleep at night. The inability to fall asleep or lack of sleep is referred to as **insomnia**.

Sleep-pattern disturbances can be categorized as a person's difficulty in falling asleep, their poor quality of sleep, and frequent awakenings, whether in the middle of the night or in the early morning.

When to Take Sleep-Aid Products

Sleep disturbances can be transient (lasting only days), short-term (lasting less than three weeks), or chronic (long-lasting). Sleep disturbances may be caused by a change in stress level. Generally, **transient insomnia** will last only a few days and does not require treatment. Short-term insomnia may be treated quite effectively with OTC sleep-aid products.

Chronic insomnia is much more severe in that it lasts longer and affects the body significantly more than short-term or transient insomnia. Chronic insomnia may be due to psychological disturbances, chronic illness, alcoholism, medication use or abuse, or many other factors. **Chronic insomnia should never be treated with OTC sleep-aid products,** and should only be treated by a physician.

Lack of sleep affects people differently, but it commonly affects their overall sense of well-being. People report that they feel tired or fatigued, overwhelmed, more sensitive, and "stressed-out" when they do not have enough sleep. In more severe cases, such as with chronic insomnia, more serious problems may occur. If left untreated, chronic insomnia can lead to physical and psychological problems as well as personality disorders.

Before choosing a sleep-aid product, many techniques can be tried to achieve sleep. These include:

◀ Caffeine intake should be minimal and avoided late in the afternoon and at night
◀ Avoid alcohol and nicotine late in the afternoon and at night
◀ Strenuous exercise should be avoided two to three hours prior to bedtime
◀ Naps should be eliminated during the day
◀ Bedtime snacks should be eliminated
◀ Bedtime should be the same each night
◀ Minimize light and noise at bedtime

It is also important to have a **wind-down ritual** before bedtime. This time should be spent doing something relaxing such as reading a book, having a light massage, lounging in your favorite chair, or bathing.

It was once believed that drinking a glass of warm milk at bedtime would actually help a person to go to sleep. However, research has shown that this simply is not true. In fact, a chemical called tryptophan that actually disturbs sleep is found in warm milk.

Go to bed with a clear mind! Many people worry about their jobs, relationships, health, etc. Worrying can actually make it difficult for you to sleep. Write these cares and concerns down on a piece of paper. This process of "dumping" your mind of worries often helps to eliminate them.

Remember that a bed is a bed. Do not use your bed as an office, study room, or place to watch television. This tends to take away from the very fact that a bed is intended as a place to sleep.

Finally, once you have gone to bed, **stay there!** If your sleep is disturbed, do not get up and start any mental or physical activities. This will only serve to make you more alert and more awake.

If these techniques fail and sleep disturbances persist, sometimes it may help if you take an OTC sleep-aid medication for short-term relief. Consult your Eckerd Pharmacist or physician before self-medicating if you are pregnant, taking any medications (prescription or non-prescription), or have any chronic illness or disease.

If an OTC medication is used for more than seven (7) to ten (10) days and your sleep is still disturbed, contact your physician before continuing its use. You may need to be examined for a more severe problem or underlying cause for your sleep disturbance.

Which OTC Sleep-Aid Is Best for YOU?

Currently, there are only two active ingredients available in OTC sleep-aid medications. These ingredients are the antihistamines **diphenhydramine** and **doxylamine.**

Many OTC analgesic (pain-relieving) or anti-fever products are also marketed as products that promote sleep. These are products that contain aspirin or acetaminophen (Tylenol™) and have a sleep-aid added to enhance their appeal. If mild pain symptoms are present or more pronounced at bedtime, these combination medications can be quite effective. Not only will they eliminate the pain, but they will help you to sleep.

Avoid these products if you have been told by your physician or pharmacist not to take medications that contain aspirin or acetaminophen due to your medical history, allergies, illness, or other medications. Table 5-1 (page 85) lists the OTC sleep-aid products that are currently available in your Eckerd Pharmacy.

Stimulant Products: What Are They and When Should You Take Them?

Stimulant products are intended to **maintain alertness** or **prevent sleep.** Currently, the only ingredient available in OTC products that is intended for alertness is **caffeine.** The amount of caffeine needed to provide stimulation varies greatly from one person to another. Many foods and beverages such as soft drinks, chocolate, coffee, and tea contain caffeine, and many medications contain caffeine as well.

When caffeine is taken in the proper amount it has been shown to be effective in increasing alertness and decreasing drowsiness. However, if too much caffeine is taken, it can cause irritability, headache, nervousness, tremors, heart palpitations, diarrhea, vomiting, and nausea. If any of these problems occur, discontinue its use immediately. It is easy to consume too much caffeine when taking these OTC stimulant products since caffeine is often consumed through our normal daily intake of foods and beverages.

Many people believe that caffeine (for example, in coffee) can be used to help "sober" a person who has consumed too much alcohol. This simply is not true. Caffeine will not counteract the effects of alcohol.

Women with severe pre-menstrual syndrome (PMS) or who have benign breast disease, fibrocystic disease, or mastitis should avoid the intake of caffeine altogether. It has been reported that the combination of caffeine use with these breast disorders can produce increased tenderness, pain, and benign cysts.

Table 5-2 (page 85) lists the most common OTC stimulant products currently available for use.

As with any medication, if you are pregnant, nursing, have a chronic illness or disease, or take other medications, consult your Eckerd Pharmacist or physician before taking stimulant products. Stimulant products are intended for short-term use only.

If fatigue persists or occurs more often than you think is "normal," contact your physician.

TABLE 5-1: OTC Sleep-Aid Products

National Brand Products	Eckerd Brand Products	Antihistamine	"Other" Ingredient	Dosage Form(s)
Doan's P.M.		Diphenhy-dramine	Magnesium Salicylate	Tablet
Exedrin P.M.		Diphenhy-dramine	Acetaminophen	Caplet, Tablet, Softgel
Nytol (Regular & Extra Strength)		Diphenhy-dramine		Caplet, Tablet
Sleepinal (Regular & Maxiumum Strength)		Diphenhy-dramine		Capsule
Sominex	Sleeping Tablets	Diphenhy-dramine		Caplet, Tablet
Sominex Pain Relief		Diphenhy-dramine	Acetaminophen	Tablet
Tylenol P.M. (Regular & Extra Strength)	Non-Aspirin Relief PM Tablets	Diphenhy-dramine	Acetaminophen	Caplet, Tablet, Gelcap
Unisom	Sleep-Aid Tablets	Doxylamine		Tablet
Unisom Sleepgels (Maximum Strength)	Sleep Liqui-gels	Diphenhy-dramine		Softgel

TABLE 5-2: OTC Stimulant Products

National Brand Products	Eckerd Brand Products	Dosage Form(s)
No Doz		Chewable Tablet, Tablet
No Doz Maximum Strength	Alertness Tablets	Caplet
Ultra Pep-Back	Alertness Tablets	Tablet
Vivarin	Alertness Tablets	Caplet, Tablet

It's right at Eckerd!

Quality Eckerd Brand Products

Here's a bold statement backed by hard evidence and a complete money-back guarantee. Eckerd Brand products meet or surpass the standards of their national brand equivalents. In fact, we guarantee your complete satisfaction. If you are not completely satisfied with any Eckerd Brand item, return it to us. We will replace it free with the national brand equivalent, or refund your money in full.

Plus, in addition to the highest possible quality, Eckerd Brand products are priced an average of 30 percent less than comparable national brands.

Consider the variety, the savings and the guarantee and you have nothing to lose and everything to gain. We invite you to discover these popular Eckerd Brand products:

Eckerd Ibuprofen
Eckerd Miconazole 7 Cream
Eckerd Tussin DM
Eckerd Docusate Sodium
Eckerd Senna Laxative
Eckerd Nasal Spray
Eckerd Anti-Diarrheal Caplets

Eckerd Sea Mist Nasal Spray
Eckerd Epinephrine Mist
Eckerd Isopropyl Alcohol
Eckerd Aspirin
Eckerd Chlortrimazole Cream
Eckerd Su-Phedrin
Eckerd TRPL Antibiotic Ointment

Get updates to the information in this book at the **Eckerd Corporation Home Page** on the World Wide Web. Visit us often at **www.eckerd.com**.

Chapter Six

Choosing the Proper Ophthalmic (Eye) Product

It has been said that the eyes are the windows to the soul. When a problem occurs involving the eyes, extreme care should be used when choosing the best treatment. The eye has mechanisms of natural protection. The eyelids protect the eye from foreign particles, such as dust. Tears aid in cleansing the eye when foreign particles are present and, therefore, are also important in protection.

At times, these natural defense mechanisms may not be sufficient to totally protect the eye. Problems such as lack of tears or lubrication, swelling, itching, inflammation, irritation, or redness may result. These problems can be treated quite effectively with OTC ophthalmic or eye preparations.

Other problems such as burns, infections, ulcers, vision impairment, or particles embedded in the eye should be treated only by a physician.

Over-the-counter eye preparations are available at your pharmacy in the form of drops and ointments. When applying **drops,** the following steps should be taken:

- Wash hands well
- Tilt the head back
- Create a "pocket" in the eye by carefully pulling the outer lower eyelid away from the eye
- Place the dropper tip above the eye and, while looking up, carefully squeeze or have someone else squeeze one drop into the eye. Next, look downward for a few seconds
- Avoid touching the dropper with the eye or finger
- Release the eyelid
- Gently close the eyes for at least three minutes
- Place gentle pressure on the inner corner of the eye with your index finger
- With a tissue, blot the excess drops from around the eyes
- If more than one drop is necessary, wait five minutes between drops

A normal eye dropper delivers more liquid than the eye can actually retain. Some excess is normal.

Some people have extreme difficulty in administering eye drops correctly. If the method described above seems too difficult, the **closed-eye method** may be used. It requires lying down and placing the drops on the closed eyelid—in the inner corner of the eye—then slowly opening the eye. Gravity will cause the drop(s) to fall into the eye.

When applying an eye **ointment,** the procedure is very different. The following steps should be followed:

- Wash hands well
- Tilt the head back
- Gently pull the lower outer eyelid below the lashes away from the eye
- Position the ointment tube over the eye
- Gently squeeze the tube and place $1/4$- to $1/2$-inch of ointment inside the lower lid
- Release the eyelid
- Gently close the eyes for a couple of minutes
- With a tissue, blot the excess ointment from around the eyes
- Blurred vision may result, but only temporarily

It is very important to follow these steps when applying either form of eye preparation to assure the best results. If you are instructed to use an ointment or prescription **eye gel** in addition to drops, always apply the drops first and then wait 10 minutes before applying the eye ointment or Rx ophthalmic gel.

Good eye hygiene is of the utmost importance! Washing your hands with an anti-bacterial soap is a good idea before you touch the area around the eyes or the eyes themselves. Children often rub their eyes when they become tired and, therefore, should be taught that frequent, thorough handwashing is a necessity.

Products are also available at your Eckerd Pharmacy that are designed to cleanse the eye area. A cotton-tipped applicator is very helpful when using these products.

Eye Conditions and Their Causes

The eyelid is an area of the eye that can often become inflamed, red, itchy, or scaly. These symptoms can be caused by a variety of factors.

The ingredients (dyes, preservatives, etc.) that are found in face make-up such as foundation, powder, or eye products (mascara, eyeliner), often cause allergic reactions. If an allergic reaction does occur, it will usually affect both eyes. It is important to replace make-up that has been used for three or more months with a new product, because the old product may become contaminated once it is exposed to air or human contact.

Definitely throw away any product that you suspect may be causing this reaction. Cold compresses or oral antihistamines (see Chapter 1 for a complete list of antihistamines) will help to minimize the allergic symptoms.

Blepharitis is a chronic condition of the eyelid producing scaly, inflamed, itchy, burning, redness, and even loss of eyelashes. This condition quite often recurs in people who have been diagnosed with blepharitis. Warm compresses applied to the eye(s) for 15 to 20 minutes, followed by lid hygiene products, such as Ocusoft Lid Scrubs™, are effective in treating these symptoms. If the symptoms persist or become more severe, then a prescription ophthalmic antibiotic preparation may be needed. Your eye physician will need to prescribe a medication for you.

Occasionally, **dust** or other **particles** will enter the eye. Tears will usually wash these particles away. If tears do not seem to adequately remove the particles, then an eye wash may be helpful. Old fashioned eye cups are not recommended because they are often a source for potential contamination. If improvement is not seen after using an eye wash, contact your physician.

Conjunctivitis is another disorder of the eye. Although conjunctivitis can be viral, bacterial, allergic, or chlamydial, the most common form is viral. Viral conjunctivitis is often referred to as **pink eye** because the eyes usually become very pink in appearance. Other symptoms include blurred vision, discomfort or pain in the eye(s), a feeling of "something" actually being in the eye(s), possibly fever, and a watery discharge from the eye(s).

Do not self-treat if the discharge is thick or mucous-like; contact your physician. Pink eye is extremely **contagious.** Good hygiene is very important. **Never** use anyone else's eye drops or ointment! Pink eye usually lasts about two weeks and will usually resolve itself. Treatment involves artificial tears or lubricant preparations and ophthalmic decongestants. If symptoms persist or seem to worsen, contact your physician. There are times when pink eye should be treated with a prescription eye product such as an antibiotic (with or without a steroid).

Perhaps the most common ophthalmic complaint involves **dry eyes.** This may be caused by medication, aging, illness, or a variety of other causes. The best treatment is with an artificial tear product. Some contain preservatives to help keep the product free of contaminants. These preservatives may cause an allergic reaction. If a reaction does occur, discontinue use and use a preservative-free product.

Many ophthalmic products are preservative-free and seem to produce the best results in the treatment of dry eyes. Often the letters **"PF"** will appear in the name of the product or **"preservative-free"** will be advertised on the box itself. They are often packaged as single-use dispensers. For example, one box may contain 30 individual applications. This enables you to use one application, discard it, and have a fresh one for the next dose. These products are available in both drop and ointment form. Use the drop form during the daytime, since the ointment may temporarily cause blurred vision. The ointment is best for nighttime use and actually stays on contact with the eye longer than the drops.

If you wear **contact lenses,** particularly soft contacts, and experience blurred vision or sensitivity to light, contact your physician immediately.

Treating the Symptoms of Eye Conditions

Table 6-1 (page 92) outlines symptoms associated with eye conditions and the medication-type best suited for their treatment.

What Are the Main Ingredients In OTC Eye Products?

Table 6-2 (page 92) outlines the main ingredients found in OTC eye preparations, their effect on the eye, side effects, and use.

Table 6-3 on page 93 identifies brand-name products, their main ingredient, use, and dosage form. Decongestant eye products that are referred to as "moisturizing" or "plus" usually have an added lubricant to help prevent drying of the eyes.

Once you have decided on the type of medication needed (artificial tears, for example) choose which product is best for you based on price, dosage form, and extra ingredients (preservative-free, for example).

If you are unsure which product is best for you, contact your Eckerd Pharmacist or your physician. If no improvement is experienced within three days, consult your physician.

Note: Sensitivity to ophthalmic decongestants is possible. Naphazoline (0.012%) may be tolerated better and may reduce the chance for **rebound congestion.** Rebound congestion is severe congestion caused by the excessive use of topical ophthalmic decongestants.

Summary

Many products are available as OTC ophthalmic medications. Choosing the one that is best for you can be confusing and time-consuming. It is important to identify your symptoms and choose the type of product best suited for your needs.

Some ophthalmic decongestants can be quite drying and, therefore, have moisturizers or lubricants added to soothe dryness. Other products are marked "preservative-free" which may be attractive to you in terms of lessening your possible allergic reactions.

When you use a topical ophthalmic preparation, be certain you follow the steps involved and described in this chapter for proper administration.

Carefully check the expiration date of the medication and do not use past the expiration date. Do not use products if they have become cloudy, changed color, or contain particles such as crystals or sediment. Do not use products for a period of more than 72 hours. If symptoms still persist after this time period, contact your physician.

If you are currently taking or using other ophthalmic medications, or if you have any medical illness such as **diabetes, high blood pressure, glaucoma,** and so forth, contact your physician before using any OTC eye medication. Do not self-treat!

TABLE 6-1: Common Eye Conditions and Products Used to Treat Them

Eye Condition and Symptoms	Type of Product Needed for Treatment
Blepharitis	Warm compresses followed by lid-hygiene or cleansing products
Eye allergies: Redness, swelling, itchy, scaly eyelids	Oral antihistamines and cold compresses
Dust or lint in eyes Irritant in eyes (example, Shampoo)	Eye wash
Conjunctivitis	Artificial tears Decongestant eye drops
Dry eyes: Itching, red, tired eyes, may feel like dust is in eyes	Artificial tears Lubricant eye products (non-medicated ointments)

TABLE 6-2: Active Ingredients in OTC Eye Products and Their Side Effects

Active Ingredient	Side Effect(s)
Lubricants: —Artificial tears —Non-medicated ointments	—Some contain preservatives that may cause allergic reaction. —Some contain preservatives that may cause allergic reaction. Ointments may cause blurred vision.
Decongestants: —Phenylephrine —Naphazoline —Tetrahydrozoline —Oxymetazoline	—Dilates pupils. Condition will worsen with prolonged use. May cause dryness of eyes. —Dilates pupils. May cause dryness of eyes. —Slight stinging. May cause dryness of eyes. —May cause dryness of eyes.
Eye washes	

TABLE 6-3: OTC Artificial Tears

National Brand Products	Active Ingredients	Dosage Form(s)
Bion Tears	Hydroxypropyl Methylcellulose	Drops
Celluvisc	Carboxymethylcellulose	Drops
Dry Eye Therapy	Glycerin	Drops
Duolube	Petrolatum Mineral Oil	Ointment
Hypotears	Polyvinyl Alcohol	Drops
Hypotears	Petrolatum	Ointment
Hypotears PF	Polyvinyl Alcohol	Drops
Murine Lubricating	Polyvinyl Alcohol	Drops
Ocucoat PF	Hydroxypropyl Methylcellulose	Drops
Ocurest (Tears)	Hydroxypropyl Methylcellulose	Drops
Refresh	Polyvinyl Alcohol	Drops
Refresh Plus Cellufresh	Carboxymethylcellulose	Drops
Teargen II	Hydroxypropyl Methylcellulose	Drops
Tears Naturale	Hydroxypropyl Methylcellulose	Drops
Tears Naturale Free	Hydroxypropyl Methylcellulose	Drops
Tears Naturale II	Hydroxypropyl Methylcellulose	Drops

TABLE 6-4: OTC Ophthalmic Decongestant Products

National Brand Products	Eckerd Brand Products	Active Ingredients	Dosage Form(s)
Allerest Eye Drops		Naphazoline (0.012%)	Drops
Clear Eyes		Naphazoline (0.012%)	Drops
Murine Plus	Eye Drops (Irritation Relief)	Tetrahydrozoline (0.05%)	Drops
Naphcon-A		Naphazoline (0.025%)	Drops
Ocu Clear		Oxymetazoline (0.025%)	Drops
Ocurest (Redness Reliever)		Tetrahydrozoline (0.05%)	Drops
Opcon-A		Naphazoline (0.027%)	Drops
Prefrin Liquifilm		Phenylephrine (0.12%)	Drops
Sensitive Eyes (Regular & Extra Strength)		Naphazoline (0.025%)	Drops
Visine A.R. Formula	Eye Drops (Irritation Relief)	Tetrahydrozoline (0.05%)	Drops
Visine L.R.		Oxymetazoline (0.025%)	Drops
Visine Moisturizing	Eye Drops (Extra Moisture)	Tetrahydrozoline (0.05%)	Drops
Visine Original	Original Eye Drops (Redness Relief)	Tetrahydrozoline (0.05%)	Drops

TABLE 6-5: OTC Eye Wash Products

National Brand Products
Aquasite Drops
Collyrium for Fresh Eyes
OcuClenz Liquid

It's right at Eckerd!

Watching the Warning Signs of Diabetes

If one or more of these Warning Signs are present, they could indicate the presence of diabetes, and you should consult your doctor.

◀ Increased thirst and urination
◀ Large amounts of sugar in the blood or urine
◀ Ketones in urine
◀ Weakness, abdominal pains, generalized aches
◀ Heavy, labored breathing
◀ Loss of appetite, nausea, and vomiting

If diabetes has been diagnosed, you can look to your Eckerd Pharmacy as your complete Diabetic Supply Headquarters. Our goal is to help you make living with diabetes easier.

To that end, we have the products and information you need. Each Eckerd Pharmacy carries a full line of insulin, foods and products to help you treat yourself at home. We invite you to shop and compare.

Get updates to the information in this book at the **Eckerd Corporation Home Page** on the World Wide Web. Visit us often at **www.eckerd.com.**

Chapter Seven

Choosing the Proper Anti-Emetic or Emetic Product

It is hard to believe that anything involving **vomiting** or the need to vomit can be important to your health. However, vomiting is an important mechanism of the body that is necessary to rid the body of accidental ingestion of **poisons** or **toxins.** It is a very unpleasant experience and involves many parts of the body. There is a "vomiting control center" in the brain that triggers the process and sets off a series of reactions that ultimately end in the act of vomiting.

The act of vomiting is known as **emesis.** Products to control emesis include both **anti-emetics** as well as **emetics.** Anti-emetics prevent nausea and vomiting. Emetics, on the other hand, induce or cause vomiting.

Vomiting may be a response to hormonal changes (example, pregnancy), motion sickness, allergies, overeating, or illness. Anti-emetic medications are very helpful for short-term relief of symptoms.

Note: If symptoms include blood in the vomitus, abdominal pain, symptoms of dehydration, fever, severe headache, weight loss of greater than 5% of the total body weight, or nausea for more than two days, consult your physician immediately for treatment.

Types of Anti-Emetic OTC Medications

Many products are available over-the-counter (OTC) that are indicated to prevent or treat nausea. These products vary greatly in cost, effectiveness, taste, route of administration, dosing frequency, and side effects.

The most common ingredients used in OTC anti-emetic products include antacids, antihistamines, carbohydrate (sugar) solutions, and bismuth salts. Table 7-1 (page 105) lists these ingredients as well as their mechanism of action, common side effects, and any general warnings about their use.

Always read the label on the product carefully for any warnings that may apply directly to you. If you have any questions about the use of these medications, please consult your Eckerd Pharmacist or physician. This chart will be helpful when choosing which medication is best for you.

Antihistamines

The most common type of OTC products that are used as anti-emetics contain antihistamines. Antihistamines commonly cause **drowsiness.** Knowing this fact is important when mental alertness is needed. Other possible side effects that may occur with antihistamine use include dry mouth, constipation, or difficulty in urinating.

Always read the label carefully before self-medicating. There are many people who should not take antihistamines due to disease, other medications, or illness. If these products are used to prevent nausea (example, nausea associated with motion), the dose should be given 30 to 60 minutes prior to travel since these products take about 30 to 60 minutes to become effective. Table 7-2 (page 105) shows the common OTC antihistamine-type anti-emetics that are available at your Eckerd Pharmacy.

Antacids

Antacids are also commonly taken when nausea is present. Nausea may be caused by excessive amounts of acid in the stomach. Antacids (see Chapter 3 for a complete listing) will help to neutralize the acid, thus eliminating the "upset stomach" that often accompanies nausea.

Carbohydrate (Sugar) Solutions

Carbohydrate (sugar) solutions can also be given to treat nausea. When taking one of these products it is important to carefully read and follow the directions for use to ensure the best results. These products should be taken at **full strength** and not diluted. Water or other fluids should be avoided before the medication has been given and for 15 minutes after. The dose may need to be repeated if nausea persists. Do not exceed the maximum dose suggested by the manufacturer.

Diabetics or people with carbohydrate-restricted (sugar-restricted) diets should not take these products due to their high sugar content. Table 7-3 (page 106) identifies the most common carbohydrate solution products that are available at your Eckerd Pharmacy.

Bismuth Salts

Bismuth-containing products are most commonly used for indigestion or to control diarrhea, but they can give some relief for symptoms of nausea as well as abdominal (stomach) cramping.

These products contain **aspirin** or aspirin-like ingredients and should not be used by people who are allergic to aspirin, have ulcers, take blood thinners (example, Coumadin), have a bleeding disorder, or have been warned by their doctor not to take aspirin. Table 7-4 (page 106) shows the common OTC bismuth salt-type anti-emetic.

Keep Your Body Well Hydrated!

One of the dangers of vomiting is the rapid loss of fluid which can quickly lead to dehydration. The symptoms of dehydration may include dry mouth, sunken eyes, weakness, low urinary output, and dizziness. This can occur **frequently** and **rapidly.** **Rehydration** fluids are available to replace lost fluid. They contain such electrolytes as sodium, chloride, potassium, and bicarbonate as well as glucose or some other sugar. They help to promote a sense of well being by replacing lost fluids and electrolytes which may occur after vomiting or diarrhea.

Keep these products on hand. They often have a long shelf life and you will be glad that you have them if and when you need them. Table 7-5 (page 106) shows the common OTC rehydration fluids that are available at your Eckerd pharmacy.

Summary

Anti-emetic products are generally quite safe and effective for relieving the symptoms of nausea.

They are intended for short term relief only. Remember, if symptoms include blood in the vomitus, abdominal pain, symptoms of dehydration, fever, severe headache, weight loss of greater than 5% of the total body weight, or nausea for more than two days, consult your physician immediately for treatment. The nausea may represent a more serious underlying problem.

Types of OTC Emetic Products

Emetic products are used to **induce vomiting** when poisonous or toxic ingredients have been ingested. However, there are times when vomiting a poisonous substance may actually cause more damage. This can occur when a substance such as acid has been swallowed and the vomiting process would actually re-expose the gastrointestinal tract to the substance.

Therefore, special precautions must be given when a poisoning has occurred.

> **Note: <u>ALWAYS CALL 911</u> or the poison control center nearest you to determine the best treatment or action.**

When calling for help for a possible poisoning, there are important facts to have ready. Having this information will ensure that you receive the fastest and most accurate help possible. The following information about the person who has ingested the poisoning will be requested:

- Name of the patient
- Address or location of patient
- Weight of patient
- Age of patient
- Product ingested (have container nearby, if possible, to read ingredients)
- Time of ingestion
- Amount ingested
- Overall health of patient (illnesses, other medications, symptoms)

Staying as calm as possible so you can answer all questions completely and clearly helps you, the patient, and the person you are speaking with give the best and quickest aid possible.

The most common OTC product available is **Syrup of Ipecac™**. Anyone living with small children needs to keep ipecac in the first-aid kit. If the poison center or 911 operator instructs you to give ipecac, there are a few things to remember:

(1) give the proper dose of ipecac
(2) follow dose with a large glass of fluid, preferably water
(3) if vomiting has not occurred within 20 minutes, give the dose again.
(4) If you are instructed to use the ipecac and then follow-up with a hospital or doctor's visit, do not wait to see if the ipecac will work. Give the ipecac, take a bucket and be on your way.

Never assume that ipecac is the best choice for treating a poisoning. For example, if a long period of time has elapsed since the poison was taken, the body will have already absorbed much of the poison and vomiting will not remove what has already been absorbed. Always call for help before giving ipecac or when there is any chance of poisoning.

Most importantly, always keep the telephone number of a poison control center near your telephone and in your purse or wallet. You never know when you might need it.

Having this telephone number ready can mean the difference between life and death. Call your poison control center. They will often send you stickers to place on or near your telephone that have their telephone number printed on them. Most importantly, don't take chances. The poison control center is there to help you!

Below is a list of certified or regional poison centers as provided by the American Association of Poison Control Centers. If your state does not appear, call the certified or regional poison center nearest you.

ALABAMA
Alabama Poison Center, Tuscaloosa
408-A Paul Bryant Drive
Tuscaloosa, AL 35401
Emergency Phone:
(800) 462–0800 (AL only)
or (205) 345–0600
Regional Poison Control Center
The Children's Hospital of Alabama
1600 7th Ave. South
Birmingham, AL 35233–1711
Emergency Phone:
(205) 939–9201, (205) 933–4050,
or (800) 292–6678 (AL only)

ARIZONA
Arizona Poison and Drug
Information Center
Arizona Health Sciences Center;
Rm. #1156
1501 N. Campbell Ave.
Tucson, AZ 85724
Emergency Phone:
(800) 362–0101 (AZ only)
or (520) 626–6016
Samaritan Regional Poison Center
Good Samaritan Regional Medical
Center
Ancillary–1
1111 E. McDowell Road
Phoenix AZ 85006
Emergency Phone: (602) 253–3334

CALIFORNIA
Central California Regional Poison
Control Center

Valley Children's Hospital
3151 N. Millbrook, IN31
Fresno, CA 93703
Emergency Phone:
(800) 346–5922 (Central CA only)
or (209) 445–1222
San Diego Regional Poison Center
UCSD Medical Center
200 West Arbor Drive
San Diego, CA 92103–8925
Emergency Phone:
(619) 543–6000 or (800) 876–4766
(in 619 area code only)
University of California, Davis,
Medical Center Regional Poison
Control Center
2315 Stockton Blvd.
Sacramento, CA 95817
Emergency Phone:
(916) 734–3692 or (800) 342–9293
(Northern California only)
San Francisco Bay Area Regional
Poison Control Center
SF General Hospital
1001 Potrero Avenue
Building 80, Room 230
San Francisco, CA 94110
Emergency Phone:
(800) 523–2222 (N. Ca.),
(800) 286–0763 or (800) 479–0944
Santa Clara Valley Regional Poison
Control Center
Valley Health Center, Suite 280
828 South Bascom Avenue
San Jose, CA 95128

Emergency Phone:
(800) 662–9886 (CA only)
COLORADO
Rocky Mountain Poison and Drug
Center
8802 E. 9th Avenue
Denver, CO 80220–6800
Emergency Phone:
(303) 629–1123
CONNECTICUT
Connecticut Regional Poison Center
University of Connecticut Health
Center
263 Farmington Avenue
Farmington, CT 06030
Emergency Phone:
(800) 343–2722 (CT only);
(860) 679–3056
DISTRICT OF COLUMBIA
National Capital Poison Ctr.
3201 New Mexico Avenue, NW,
Suite 310
Washington, DC 20016
Emergency Phone:
(202) 625–3333 or (202) 362–8563
(TTY)
FLORIDA
Florida Poison Information Center
Miami
University of Miami, School of
Medicine
Department of Pediatrics
P.O. Box 016960 (R–131)
Miami, FL 33101
Emergency Number:
(800) 282–3171 (FL only)
Florida Poison Information Center
Jacksonville
University Medical Center
University of Florida Health Science
Center Jacksonville
655 West 8th Street
Jacksonville, FL 32009
Emergency Phone:
(800) 282–3171 (FL only) or
(904) 549–4480
The Florida Poison Information
Center and Toxicology Resource
Center
Tampa General Hospital
P.O. Box 1289
Tampa, FL 33601
Emergency Phone:
(800) 282–3171 (Florida) or
(813) 253–4444 (Tampa)
GEORGIA
Georgia Poison Center
Grady Memorial Hospital
80 Butler Street S. E.

P.O. Box 26066
Atlanta, GA 30335–3801
Emergency Phone:
(800) 282–5846 (GA only)
or (404) 616–9000
INDIANA
Indiana Poison Center
Methodist Hospital of Indiana
1701 N. Senate Boulevard
P.O. Box 1367
Indianapolis, IN 46206–1367
Emergency Phone:
(800) 382–9097 (IN only)
or (317) 929–2323
KENTUCKY
Kentucky Regional Poison Center of
Kosair Children's Hospital
Medical Towers South, Suite 572
P.O. Box 35070
Louisville, KY 40232–5070
Emergency Phone:
(800) 722–5725 (KY only)
or (502) 629–7275
LOUISIANA
Louisiana Drug and Poison
Information Center
Northeast Louisiana University
Sugar Hall
Monroe, LA 71209–6430
Emergency Phone:
(800) 256–9822 or (318) 362–5393
MARYLAND
Maryland Poison Center
20 N. Pine St.
Baltimore, MD 21201
Emergency Phone:
(800) 492–2414 (MD only)
or (410) 528–7701
National Capital Poison Center
(D.C. suburbs only)
3201 New Mexico Avenue, NW,
Suite 310
Washington, DC 20016
Emergency Phone:
(202) 625–3333 or (202) 362–8563
(TTY)
MASSACHUSETTS
Massachusetts Poison Control System
300 Longwood Ave.
Boston, MA 02115
Emergency Phone:
(800) 682–9211 or (617) 232–2120
MICHIGAN
Poison Control Center
Children's Hospital of Michigan
4160 John Rd., Suite 425
Detroit, MI 48201
Emergency Phone:
(313) 745–5711

MINNESOTA

Hennepin Regional Poison Center
Hennepin County Medical Center
701 Park Ave.
Minneapolis, MN 55415
Emergency Phone:
(612) 347–3141 or Petline:
(612) 337–7387 or TDD
(612) 337–7474

Minnesota Regional Poison Center
8100 34th Avenue S.
P.O. Box 1309
Minneapolis, MN 55440–1309
Emergency Phone:
(612) 221–2113

MISSOURI

Cardinal Glennon Children's Hospital
Regional Poison Center
1465 S. Grand Blvd.
St. Louis, MO 63104
Emergency Phone:
(800) 366–8888 or (314) 772–5200

MONTANA

Residents of Montana call the following:
Rocky Mountain Poison and Drug
Center
8802 E. 9th Avenue
Denver, CO 80220
Emergency Phone:
(303) 629–1123

NEBRASKA

The Poison Center
8301 Dodge St.
Omaha, NE 68114
Emergency Phone:
(800) 955–9119 (NE & WY)
or (402) 390–5555 (Omaha)

NEW JERSEY

New Jersey Poison Information
and Education System
201 Lyons Ave.
Newark, NJ 07112
Emergency Phone:
(800) 764–7661 (NJ only),
(201) 926–8008

NEW MEXICO

New Mexico Poison and Drug
Information Center
University of New Mexico
Health Sciences Library, Room 125
Albuquerque, NM 87131–1076
Emergency Phone:
(800) 432–6866 (NM only)
or (505) 843–2551

NEW YORK

Central New York Poison Control
Center

SUNY Health Science Center
750 E. Adams Street
Syracuse, NY 13203
Emergency Phone:
(800) 252–5655 (NY only)
or (315) 476–4766

Finger Lakes Regional Poison Center
University of Rochester Medical
Center
601 Elmwood Avenue
Box 321, Room G–3275
Rochester, NY 14642
Emergency Phone:
(800) 333–0542 or (716) 275–5151

Hudson Valley Regional Poison
Center
Phelps Memorial Hospital Center
701 North Broadway
North Tarrytown, NY 10591
Emergency Phone:
(800) 336–6997 or (914) 366–3030

Long Island Regional Poison Control
Center
Winthrop University Hospital
259 First Street
Mineola, NY 11501
Emergency Phone:
(516) 542–2323

New York City Poison Control Center
N.Y.C. Department of Health
455 First Ave., Room 123
New York, NY 10016
Emergency Phone:
(212) 340–4494,
or TDD (212) 689–9014

NORTH CAROLINA

Carolinas Poison Center
1012 S. Kings Drive, Suite 206
P.O. Box 32861
Charlotte, NC 28232–2861
Emergency Phone:
(800) 848–6946 or (704) 355–4000

OHIO

Central Ohio Poison Center
700 Children's Drive
Columbus, OH 43205–2696
Emergency Phone:
(800) 682–7625, (614) 228–1323
or (614) 228–2272 (TTY),
(614) 461–2012

Cincinnati Drug & Poison
Information Center and Regional
Poison Control System
P.O. Box 670144
Cincinnati, OH 45267–0144
Emergency Phone:
(800) 872–5111 (OH only)
or (513) 558–5111

OREGON
Oregon Poison Center
Oregon Health Sciences University
3181 S.W. Sam Jackson Park
Road, CB550
Portland, OR 97201
Emergency Phone:
(800) 452-7165 (OR only)
or (503) 494-8968

PENNSYLVANIA
Central Pennsylvania Poison Center
University Hospital
Milton S. Hershey Medical Center
Hershey, PA 17033
Emergency Phone:
(800) 521-6110
The Poison Control Center
3600 Sciences Center, Suite 220
Philadelphia, PA 19104-2641
Emergency Phone:
(215) 386-2100
Pittsburgh Poison Center
3705 Fifth Avenue
Pittsburgh, PA 15213
Emergency Phone:
(412) 681-6669

RHODE ISLAND
Rhode Island Poison Center
593 Eddy St.
Providence, RI 02903
Emergency Phone:
(401) 444-5727

TENNESSEE
Middle Tennessee Poison Center
The Center for Clinical Toxicology
Vanderbilt University Medical Center
1161 21st Avenue South
501 Oxford House
Nashville, TN 37232-4632
Emergency Phone:
(800) 288-9999 or (615) 936-2034

TEXAS
Central Texas Poison Center
Scott & White Memorial Hospital
2401 S. 31st Street
Temple, TX 76508
Emergency Phone:
(800) 764-7661
North Texas Poison Center
5201 Harry Hines Blvd.
P.O. Box 35926
Dallas, TX 75235
Emergency Phone:
(800) 764-7661; Texas Watts
(800) 441-0040
Southeast Texas Poison Center
The University of Texas Medical
Branch
301 University Avenue

Galveston, TX 77550-2780
Emergency Phone:
(409) 765-1420 (Galveston),
(713) 654-1701 (Houston):
(800) 764-7661

UTAH
Utah Poison Control Center
410 Chipeta Way, Suite 230
Salt Lake City, UT 84108
Emergency Phone:
(800) 456-7707 (UT only)
or (801) 581-2151

VIRGINIA
Blue Ridge Poison Center
Box 67, Blue Ridge
University of Virginia Medical
Center
Charlottesville, VA 22901
Emergency Phone:
(800) 451-1428 or (804) 924-5543
National Capital Poison Center
(Northern VA only)
3201 New Mexico Avenue, NW,
Suite 310
Washington, DC 20016
Emergency Phone:
(202) 625-3333
or (202) 362-8563 (TTY)

WASHINGTON
Washington Poison Center
155 N.E. 100th Street, Suite #400
Seattle, WA 98125
Emergency Phone:
(206) 526-2121, (800) 732-6985,
(800) 572-0638 (TDD only)
or (206) 517-2394

WEST VIRGINIA
West Virginia Poison Center
3110 MacCorkle Ave., S. E.
Charleston, WV 25304
Emergency Phone:
(800) 642-3625 (WV only)
or (304) 348-4211

WYOMING
Residents of Wyoming call the
following:
The Poison Center
8301 Dodge St.
Omaha, NE 68114
Emergency Phone:
(800) 955-9119 (NE & WY)
or (402) 390-5555 (Omaha)

TABLE 7-1: Ingredients in OTC Anti-Emetic Products

Ingredient	Side Effects	Mechanism of Action	Purpose	Warnings
Antacids	Diarrhea Constipation	Neutralize stomach acid	Relieve upset stomach	Use care when taking other medications at the same time
Antihistamines	Drowsiness Dry mouth Blurred vision	Depress labyrinth excitability	Used for motion sickness (take 30–60 min. before travel)	Avoid alcohol
Carbohydrate (Sugar) Solution	Diarrhea Stomach pain	Inhibits gastric emptying	Relieve upset stomach	Diabetics should not use
Bismuth Salts	Stomach upset	"Coating" effect on the stomach lining	Relieve gas, heartburn, and upset stomach	May contain aspirin. Black tongue or stool may be seen. Children with viral symptoms should not use.

TABLE 7-2: Antihistamine-Type OTC Anti-Emetic Products

National Brand Products	Eckerd Brand Products	Main Ingredient	Dosage Form(s)
Bonine		Meclizine	Chewable Tablet
Dramamine	Motion Sickness Tabs	Dimen-hydrinate	Tablet, Liquid
Dramamine II	Motion Sickness II Tabs	Dimen-hydrinate	Tablet
Nausene		Diphen-hydramine	Tablet
Triptone	Motion Sickness Tabs	Dimen-hydrinate	Tablet

TABLE 7-3: Carbohydrate Solution Products Used as Anti-Emetcis

National Brand Products	Eckerd Brand Products	Dosage Form(s)
Emetrol	Anti-Nausea Liquid	Liquid
Cola Syrup		Liquid

TABLE 7-4: A Bismuth Salt Product Used as an Anti-Emetic

National Brand Products	Eckerd Brand Products	Dosage Form(s)
Pepto Bismol	Pink Bismuth	Liquid, Chewable Tablet, Gelcap

TABLE 7-5: Rehydration Products Used as Anti-Emetics

National Brand Products	Eckerd Brand Products	Dosage Form(s)
Infalyte	Pediatric Electrolyte	Liquid
Kao Electrolyte	Pediatric Electrolyte	Liquid
Pedialyte	Pediatric Electrolyte	Liquid
Pedialyte		Freezer Pops

Notes Pertaining to Your Personal OTC Drug Preferences

_____

_____

_____

_____

_____

_____

_____

_____

_____

_____

_____

_____

_____

_____

_____

_____

_____

_____

_____

_____

_____

_____

It's right at Eckerd!

Visit Our Health Information Center

Information is vital to good health and proper treatment. We invite you to visit the Health Information Center at your Eckerd Pharmacy for helpful health information on various topics.

The informative booklets in our Health Information Series cover a variety of health issues. If you wish to know more about the cause or treatment of various conditions including headaches, arthritis, cholesterol, flu shots, hay fever, hypertension, pain killers, fever, diaper rash, irregularity, head lice, acne, diet, or nutrition, you will appreciate our handy, answer-filled Health Information Series.

Of course, there is no charge for these booklets and we invite you to help yourself and to share them with friends and family.

Get updates to the information in this book at the **Eckerd Corporation Home Page** on the World Wide Web. Visit us often at **www.eckerd.com.**

Chapter Eight

Choosing the Proper Anti-Bacterial or Anti-Fungal Product

The skin, the largest organ of the body, acts as a protective barrier. This barrier is necessary since the skin is exposed to the atmosphere and, therefore, many microorganisms.

When the skin becomes damaged or irritation occurs, it becomes very susceptible to infections including **bacterial, viral,** and **fungal.** Currently, viral infections can be cured only with the use of prescription medications. Bacterial and fungal infections, however, can often be treated with OTC medications and respond quite well to their use.

Bacterial skin infections are caused by an excessive amount of microorganism growth. Fungal skin infections are caused by the excessive growth of **yeast** or **mold.** Bacteria and fungus often grow faster in a warm, moist environment.

Keep Your Skin Healthy!

The ability of the skin to act as a protective organ for the body depends largely on the condition of the skin itself. Age, dehydration, damage, medications, and disease states all have an effect on the condition of the skin.

8

Having healthy skin is the best way to prevent infections. It is a must to keep the skin clean, well hydrated (by drinking lots of water), cool, and dry. When the skin becomes dehydrated, OTC topical medications cannot pass through the skin properly and will be poorly absorbed.

Many OTC medications and prescriptions have ingredients such as **petrolatum, mineral oil,** or **lanolin** added to help the skin absorb the medication as well as accumulate moisture.

It is important to remember that an infection may be a symptom of a more severe underlying problem. Your physician should be seen if the condition worsens or does not respond to treatment. Oral antibiotics or more aggressive therapy may be necessary.

Also, contact your physician if any of the following exist:

- fever
- inflammation (swelling)
- severe skin damage
- excessive oozing from the skin
- a large area is affected
- illness is present (diabetes, AIDS, etc.)
- lesions are deep
- damage is caused by an animal bite
- damage is caused by a severe burn
- anti-infectives do not improve the condition

Types of Bacterial Infections that Affect the Skin

The most common types of bacterial infections of the skin are impetigo, ecthyma, folliculitis, erysipelas, boils, and carbuncles. Often, minor scrapes or cuts on the skin will lead to redness and/or tenderness due to infection and can also be treated quite effectively with OTC topical antibiotic preparations. The common bacterial infections of the skin are discussed and described below.

Impetigo

Impetigo occurs most often in children. However, it is very contagious and can affect anyone. It is characterized by small red spots on the skin's surface that are filled with a light brown or amber fluid. These spots often develop into blister-like lesions. Eventually, yellowish-brown scabs form that are surrounded by red skin. Exposed skin is usually first affected, but because impetigo is so contagious, any skin can be affected.

A visit to a physician is often needed when impetigo is present, because oral antibiotics are often required and prescribed. In mild cases, OTC topical antibiotic products can be effective.

Before applying the medication, wash your hands and the infected area with a mild soap and water. This will help to loosen any crusts on the infected area.

Ecthyma

Ecthyma is a condition that is similar to impetigo in appearance.

However, ecthyma affects a deeper area of the skin than impetigo. It is most often seen after some trauma or injury to the skin has occurred. It first appears as pus-filled reddish elevations that eventually crust. Scar formation is possible with ecthyma.

It is important to keep the affected area dry. Moisture can make the disease much more severe. Ecthyma may respond to topical OTC antibiotic products. If rapid improvement is not seen, a physician's care is necessary.

Folliculitis

Folliculitis affects the hair follicle of the skin. Skin that is often exposed to water or oils is most affected. Folliculitis is characterized by **papules** or **pustules.** Papules are small elevations that appear around the hair follicle. Pustules are also small elevations and appear around the hair follicles, but they contain a fluid called pus.

Generally, with folliculitis, the skin surrounding the hair follicle is not affected. Folliculitis often responds well to the application of topical OTC antibiotic products.

Erysipelas

Erysipelas often affects the face and/or scalp and is caused by organisms that enter through a break in the outer surface of the skin. Once infected, elevations appear that are reddish in color and have well-defined borders. These elevations often appear wet on the surface. Fever and chills often accompany erysipelas.

Pain and/or fever reducing medications will help ease these symptoms.

The affected area often responds well to the use of OTC topical antibiotics.

Boils

Boils generally occur in or around hair follicles and appear as elevations that are red, painful, and swollen.

Pus as well as a mucous plug may form. Unlike folliculitis in which many elevations may be seen, usually only one boil will be present at one time. More serious infections may lead to ulceration or scarring. Boils that are not treated properly may develop into carbuncles if infection occurs in the surrounding area.

Note: Never attempt to lance or remove a boil. This should be done only by your physician.

Carbuncles

Carbuncles are similar to boils, but they cause damage to a deeper area of the skin. Larger surface areas are usually affected and follicles often form into clusters.

> Note: Never attempt to lance or remove carbuncles. This should be done only by your physician.

Treatment of Bacterial Skin Infections

It is important to keep the skin hydrated and clean in order to prevent infection. When infection does occur, proper treatment is a must. Decide what type of infection you have, ask your Eckerd Pharmacist for help, then choose the best treatment.

Most OTC antibiotic products will effectively cure the disorders described here. They are available in different forms (for example, creams and ointments). Creams are usually applied to areas that are easy to penetrate. Ointments should be used when the area is dry and scaly and needs to trap moisture.

Infections on the surface of the skin frequently respond well to OTC topical antibiotics. Deeper or more serious infections often require a doctor's visit since prescription medications may be necessary.

The ingredients found in OTC topical antibiotics include **bacitracin, neomycin,** or **polymyxin B**—alone or in combination. Each one of these antibiotics treats specific types of microorganisms. Therefore, a combination of the three ingredients will give a broader spectrum of coverage. However, **allergic reactions** have been reported, especially with the use of neomycin. If an allergic reaction occurs, discontinue use and try a different product that does not contain neomycin. If improvement is not seen, contact your physician.

Some OTC topical anti-infective products are combined with local anesthetics to help alleviate the pain that may be present at the site of application. Some products contain antiseptics that are added to prevent or inhibit the growth of bacteria. Products are available as antiseptics that may also aid in cleaning the area, preventing infection, and inhibiting further growth.

Table 8-1 (page 116) lists the most common topical OTC anti-infective products, their active ingredients, and dosage form(s). Since many products contain the same ingredients, it is important to consider the percentage of ingredient present and the cost. Many generics are also available in the same strength as the national brand products and often at a much lower price.

Types of Fungal Infections that Affect the Skin

The most common types of fungal infections that affect the skin are: *Tinea pedis* (athlete's foot), *Tinea cruris* (jock itch), *Tinea capitis* (scalp itch), *Tinea corporis* (ringworm), *Tinea versicolor*, and Candidiasis (vaginal yeast infection and thrush).

These infections respond well to topical OTC anti-fungal medications.

Tinea pedis

Tinea pedis, or athlete's foot, is the most commonly encountered type of fungal infection involving the skin. Symptoms may include itching, burning, stinging, odor, scaliness, and dryness. In severe conditions inflammation, oozing, weeping, and pain may be present.

Athlete's foot is most common in adults who wear closed-toe shoes and whose feet are often wet due to sweat or moisture in the shoes themselves (rain, humidity, etc.). When possible, wear well-ventilated shoes that allow for proper air flow. When athlete's foot is present, small vesicles and/or eroded areas may appear between the toes and on other surfaces of the feet.

Tinea cruris

Tinea cruris, or jock itch, affects the genital region including the inner side of the upper thighs, the perineal region, and the groin, and is accompanied by severe itching.

Red lesions often appear, and in chronic or severe cases, they may turn brown. Jock itch usually affects both sides of the body.

It is important to keep the genital area as free of moisture as possible, especially if infection occurs frequently. Moisture—especially warm moisture—increases the chance of infection.

Tinea capitis

Tinea capitis affects children more than adults and appears as various-sized patches of baldness that are scattered throughout the scalp.

Symptoms associated with *Tinea capitis* include itching and baldness. Baldness is caused by the hair shaft breaking off at the surface. Red or black dots are often seen in the exposed area. In severe cases, the lesions will become crusted and scarring is possible.

Tinea corporis

Tinea corporis is a type of ringworm (not really a worm) that affects the skin on the body. The eruptions appear as circular, red scales with severe itching. They may or may not contain pus. This infection occurs most commonly in areas with high humidity.

Tinea versicolor

Tinea versicolor most often affects the trunk of the body, but it can affect the limbs as well. It is accompanied by patches of white to tan/brown that appear scattered randomly over the area. Exposure to the sun can worsen the appearance of tinea versicolor.

This condition will often correct itself, but since it can be cosmetically unappealing, treatment is sometimes desired.

Candidiasis

Candidiasis usually affects the mouth, groin area, under the breasts, underarms and between toes or fingers, or areas that are warm and/or moist. Candidiasis of the mouth is often called **thrush.** Thrush appears as a whitish/yellow coating of the tongue or roof of the mouth. Candidiasis of the vagina is often called a **yeast infection.** Symptoms of a yeast infection include an odorous smell, discharge, or itching of the vagina.

Medications, such as antibiotics, may actually cause candidal infections. Fortunately, these types of infections respond well to topical OTC anti-fungal products.

Treatment of Fungal Skin Infections

Remember, it is important to keep the skin **hydrated** and **clean** in order to prevent infection. However, if infection does occur, prompt and proper treatment is a must.

Decide what type of infection you have (your Eckerd Pharmacist can help), then decide what is the best treatment.

Most OTC anti-fungal products effectively treat these diseases. Infections that are on the surface of the skin respond well to OTC topical anti-fungal medications. Deeper or more serious infections often require a visit to your physician since prescription medications may be necessary.

There are many dosage form(s) available in OTC anti-fungal medications. **Creams** and **solutions** are the most effective because they are massaged directly into the skin and, therefore, keep contact with the affected site better than other dosage forms such as powders or sprays.

Powders or **sprays** are most effective when used along with a cream or solution. Consider the area of the body that you will be treating when choosing the best product. Table 8-2 (page 117) lists several common OTC anti-fungal medications, their active ingredient(s), dosage form(s), and type of infection they are intended to treat. There are generic products available for many of these products and should be considered if cost is a factor.

Summary

As with any OTC medication, anti-infectives are intended for short-term self-treatment, unless otherwise directed by your physician. This is important to remember because long-term use can actually lead to what is known as a **superinfection,** which results in an excessive growth of organisms that are not susceptible to the product. This overgrowth can lead to a secondary infection. Substantial improvement should be seen after one week. If, however, a noticed improvement is not seen after initial treatment has begun, or if the infection seems to be worsening, discontinue the medication and contact your physician.

Also, if you have a fever, inflammation, severe skin damage with excessive oozing, a large affected area, illness (diabetes, AIDS, etc.) exists, or deep lesions, a physician visit is necessary. Contact your physician if the infection is due to an **animal bite** or a **severe burn.** Oral anti-infectives or more aggressive therapy may be necessary to eliminate the infection.

When preparing to apply a topical anti-infective product, it is important to thoroughly wash your hands and the affected area with a mild soap and water. Use the product only as directed on the package. Over-the-counter topical anti-infectives should never be used in or around the eyes, mouth, or nose.

Even with all of this information, skin infections may be difficult to classify as bacterial or fungal. If you are uncertain what type of infection you have, your Eckerd Pharmacist will be happy to assist you.

TABLE 8-1: Common Topical OTC
Antibiotic Combination Products

National Brand Products	Eckerd Brand Products	Active Ingredients	Dosage Form(s)
Bactine First Aid Antibiotic plus Anesthetic		Polymyxin B Bacitracin Neomycin Diperodon (Anesthetic)	Ointment
Campho-Phenique Maximum Antibiotic Plus Pain Reliever		Polymyxin B Bacitracin Neomycin Lidocaine (Anesthetic)	Ointment
Lanabiotic		Polymyxin B Bacitracin Neomycin Lidocaine (Anesthetic)	Ointment
Mycitracin		Polymyxin B Bacitracin Neomycin	Ointment
Mycitracin Plus		Polymyxin B Bacitracin Neomycin Lidocaine (Anesthetic)	Ointment
Neosporin	Antibiotic Cream	Polymyxin B Neomycin	Cream
Neosporin	Triple Antibiotic Ointment	Polymyxin B Bacitracin Neomycin	Ointment
Neosporin Plus Maximum Strength	Antibiotic Maximum Strength Cream with Lidocaine	Polymyxin B Neomycin Lidocaine (Anesthetic)	Cream
Neosporin Plus Maximum Strength	Antibiotic Maximum Strength Ointment with Lidocaine	Polymyxin B Bacitracin Neomycin Lidocaine (Anesthetic)	Ointment
Polysporin		Polymyxin B Bacitracin	Ointment, Spray

TABLE 8-2: Common Topical OTC Anti-Fungal Products

National Brand Products	Eckerd Brand Products	Active Ingredients	Dosage Form(s)	Intended to Treat
Betadine First Aid		Povidone-iodine	Cream, Spray	
Betadine		Povidone-iodine	Gel, Douche, Ointment	
Cruex Anti-fungal		Undecylenate	Spray-powder, Cream	*Tinea cruris, pedis*
Desenex Anti-fungal		Tolnaftate	Spray-liquid	*Tinea pedis, cruris, corporis, versicolor*
Desenex Anti-fungal Aerosol		Undecylenate	Spray-powder	*Tinea pedis, cruris*
Desenex Anti-fungal		Undecylenate	Cream, Ointment, Powder	*Tinea pedis, cruris*
Desenex Foot & Sneaker Deodorant Powder Plus		Undecylenate	Powder	*Tinea pedis*
Gyne-Lotrimin (Vaginal)	Clotrimazole 7 Inserts	Clotrimazole	Vaginal Inserts	Candidiasis
Gyne-Lotrimin (Vaginal)		Clotrimazole	Cream	Candidiasis
Lotrimin AF	Clotrimazole Cream	Clotrimazole	Cream	*Tinea pedis, cruris, corporis, versicolor*
Lotrimin AF Jock Itch		Clotrimazole	Spray-powder, Lotion	*Tinea cruris*
Micatin Athlete's Foot	Miconazole Cream 2%	Miconazole Nitrate	Cream	*Tinea pedis*
Monistat 7 (Vaginal)	Miconazole 7 Suppositories	Miconazole Nitrate	Vaginal Inserts	Candidiasis
Monistat 7 (Vaginal)	Miconazole 7 Cream	Miconazole Nitrate	Cream	Candidiasis
Monistat 3 (Vaginal)		Miconazole Nitrate	Vaginal Cream	Candidiasis

continued

TABLE 8-2: Common Topical OTC Anti-Fungal Products (continued)

National Brand Products	Eckerd Brand Products	Active Ingredients	Dosage Form(s)	Intended to Treat
Tinactin Cream	Athlete's Foot Cream	Tolnaftate	Cream	*Tinea pedis*
Tinactin Powder	Athlete's Foot Powder	Tolnaftate	Powder	*Tinea pedis*
Vagistat-1		Tioconazole	Ointment	Candidiasis
Zeasorb-AF		Miconazole Nitrate	Powder	*Tinea pedis, cruris, corporis, versicolor*

Notes Pertaining to Your Personal OTC Drug Preferences

_____

_____

_____

_____

_____

_____

_____

_____

_____

_____

_____

_____

_____

_____

_____

_____

_____

_____

_____

_____

_____

It's right at Eckerd!

Eckerd Means Convenience

Wherever you are, and whatever your prescription needs, an Eckerd Pharmacist is ready to provide you with personalized counseling and attention, and with unique and practical services.

First, you have the convenience of having your prescription refilled at over 2,800 Eckerd locations in 24 states.

Plus, in emergencies, when you are far away and simply not able to get to an Eckerd Pharmacy, we can ship your prescription to you anywhere in the United States—overnight! Call 1–800–557–8857.*

Get updates to the information in this book at the **Eckerd Corporation Home Page** on the World Wide Web. Visit us often at **www.eckerd.com.**

Emergency Mail Rx Delivery—Anywhere!
1-800-557-8857

* Orders received before 2:00 p.m., Monday through Friday only. Nominal charge for shipping and handling.

Chapter Nine

Choosing the Proper Hemorrhoidal Product

Hemorrhoids are abnormally large sacs of veins, tissues, and mucous membranes located in the rectal area. **Dilation** or swelling is due to the thinning and weakening of the veins' walls. This can be very uncomfortable, annoying, unpleasant, and sometimes painful. These complaints aside, hemorrhoids can be very serious.

Hemorrhoids occur most often in people between the ages of 20 and 50 and affect both males and females. They may be caused by pregnancy and labor, heavy lifting, constipation, diarrhea, excessive standing, lack of fluid or fiber in the diet, or infection. Basically, any excessive strain on the rectal area can lead to hemorrhoids. Heredity may also play a role in the development of hemorrhoids.

Hemorrhoids may be **internal, external,** or **internal-external.** As the name implies, internal hemorrhoids are found inside the anal canal. Conversely, external hemorrhoids are found around the outer rim of the anus. Internal-external hemorrhoids are a combination of these two types.

Hemorrhoidal Symptoms and Ingredients Used to Treat Them

The symptoms associated with hemorrhoids can range from mild to severe and may involve more than one symptom. It is important that you identify your symptoms and select a product that will treat all or as many of these symptoms as possible.

Below is a brief discussion of the symptoms that commonly occur with hemorrhoids and, after each description, a chart listing the ingredients that will bring relief to that symptom.

Itching

When the rectal area becomes inflamed or swollen, as it often does with hemorrhoids, a discharge of secretion occurs that leads to itching. This may also be due to many other factors. Luckily, most, if not all, OTC hemorrhoidal preparations contain an ingredient(s) to help relieve itching.

CHART 9-1: OTC Hemorrhoidal Ingredients That Relieve Itching

Aluminum Chlorhydroxyallantoinate	Juniper Oil
	Lanolin
Aluminum Hydroxide	Menthol
Benzocaine	Petrolatum
Benzyl Alcohol	Mineral Dil
Camphor	Pramoxine
Cocoa Butter	Phenylephrine
Diburaine	Hydrochloride
Dyclonine	Resorcinol
Hydrocortisone	Starch
Glycerin	Tetracaine
Kaolin	

Burning

Another common complaint associated with hemorrhoids is burning. The symptom occurs mainly as a result of superficial ulceration in the anal area. The degree of this sensation may range from a feeling of mild warmth to a feeling of on-fire.

This feeling may be constant or may worsen at certain times such as during exercise or defecation. Many OTC hemorrhoidal preparations contain an ingredient(s) to help ease this burning sensation.

CHART 9-2: OTC Hemorrhoidal Ingredients That Relieve Burning

Benzocaine	Lidocaine
Benzyl Alcohol	Pramoxine
Dibucaine	Tetracaine
Dyclonine	Tetracaine Hydrochloride

Pain

The pain associated with hemorrhoids is often due to the inflammation, swelling, infection, or protrusion of the hemorrhoid outside the anus which may interfere with sitting or walking.

Pain can range from mild to severe. If pain is severe or persistent, contact your physician and do not self-medicate. Many OTC hemorrhoidal preparations contain an ingredient(s) to help ease pain.

CHART 9-3: OTC Hemorrhoidal Ingredients That Relieve Pain

Benzocaine	Dyclonine Hydrochloride
Benzyl Alcohol	Juniper Oil
Camphor	Pramoxine Hydrochloride
Dibucaine	Tetracaine

Swelling

Swelling or inflammation often accompanies hemorrhoids and occurs when veins become engorged or when fluid accumulates in tissue around the dilated veins.

Swelling may cause pain, redness, irritation, or a burning sensation. Inflammation associated with hemorrhoids responds well to the ingredients found in several common OTC hemorrhoidal products.

CHART 9-4: OTC Hemorrhoidal Ingredients That Relieve Swelling

Calamine	Hydrocortisone
Ephedrine Sulfate	Phenylephrine
Epinephrine Base	Hydrochloride
Epinephrine Hydrochloride	Witch Hazel
	Zinc Oxide

Irritation

Irritation may be caused by all of the symptoms discussed above: itching, burning, pain, and inflammation. Many OTC hemorrhoidal preparations contain an ingredient(s) to help ease irritation.

CHART 9-5: OTC Hemorrhoidal Ingredients That Relieve Irritation

Aluminum Hydroxide	Lanolin
Benzocaine	Lidocaine
Benzyl Alcohol	Menthol
Calamine	Mineral Oil
Camphor	Petrolatum
Cocoa Butter	Pramoxine
Dibucaine	Starch
Dyclonine	Tetracaine
Glycerin	Tetracaine Hydochloride
Juniper Oil	Witch Hazel
Kaolin	Zinc Oxide

Bleeding

Weakening and dilation of the vein's walls can cause hemorrhoids to rupture easily and cause bleeding. This usually occurs during or after a bowel movement. Bleeding may range from traces of bright red spots on the toilet paper to severe drops. Do not self-treat hemorrhoids if bleeding is present. Contact your physician.

As you can see by all of these charts, one ingredient may relieve more than one symptom. For example, pramoxine appears in four different tables because it relieves symptoms of itching, burning, pain, bleeding, and irritation. The reason that these ingredients relieve more than one symptom is that one symptom is often caused by another, therefore, treating one symptom will in turn treat another.

Table 9-1 (page 127) contains the brand-name OTC hemorrhoidal products commonly found in pharmacies, their ingredients, and dosage form(s). When choosing which product is best for you, it is important to 1) properly identify your symptom(s), 2) choose which ingredients will relieve that symptom(s), 3) choose a product that contains the desired ingredient(s), and 4) decide which dosage form you feel comfortable using (example, suppository, foam, cream, etc.). Many generic brand products are also available and are usually at a much lower price.

Treating Hemorrhoids

When preparing to apply hemorrhoidal medications, it is important to first clean the affected area. This can be done by washing the rectal area with a mild soap and water, rinsing well, and gently drying the area with a soft tissue or cloth.

If this thorough washing is not possible, the area should be cleaned with a medicated wipe or pad. Medication should be applied sparingly and only as directed on the package. When possible, apply the medication after a bowel movement, rather than before.

When choosing a dosage form to treat hemorrhoids, consider their location. For example, when treating internal hemorrhoids, choose products in the form of suppositories, ointments, creams, foam, or jellies to ensure the best result.

External hemorrhoids are best treated with ointments, creams, pads, foams, lotions, or jellies.

Important: Do not insert treatment preparations into the rectum that are intended for external use only!

If hemorrhoids are accompanied by painful swelling, contain a pus-like substance, are bleeding, recur, or exist as a large mass, contact your physician. Do not self-medicate. These symptoms may indicate infection or a more serious underlying problem.

Limit self-medication of hemorrhoids to a seven-day period. If symptoms are still present after seven days, contact your physician. OTC hemorrhoidal products are intended to relieve the pain, itching, swelling, burning, and irritation that accompany hemorrhoids. A good product will contain many ingredients aimed at relieving most or all of these symptoms.

Some products can cause additional **minor irritation.** If irritation occurs, discontinue use. Other products contain warnings about their use if certain disease states (diabetes, heart disease, etc.) are present. If you are unsure about using an OTC hemorrhoidal product, talk to your Eckerd Pharmacist or physician.

Constipation often precedes or accompanies hemorrhoids. It often causes people to strain during a bowel movement, thereby aggravating the hemorrhoids. The use of bulk-forming laxatives often helps to ease this symptom. Table 9-2 (page 128) lists the most common bulk-forming laxatives. When taking this type of laxative it is important to drink plenty of fluids to ensure the best response. If you are a diabetic or on a carbohydrate-restricted diet, talk to your pharmacist or physician before taking bulk-forming laxatives.

Summary

Hemorrhoids can be quite severe and very serious. Having normal bowel movements can help to prevent hemorrhoids from occurring. A well-balanced diet, exercise, and adequate intake of fluid will help to maintain normal bowel function.

If hemorrhoids occur, they should be treated properly and promptly. Choose a product containing the ingredients that will treat your symptoms best. If hemorrhoids are accompanied with painful swelling, contain a pus-like substance, are bleeding, recur, or exist as a large mass, contact your physician. **Do not self-treat hemorrhoids for more than seven days.**

Directions on the product label must be followed. If symptoms persist after this time, contact your physician.

TABLE 9-1: Common Hemorrhoidal Products

National Brand Products	Eckerd Brand Products	Ingredient(s)	Dosage Form(s)
Americaine		Benzocaine*	Ointment, Spray
Anusol HC–1		Hydrocortisone	Ointment
Anusol		Pramoxine* Zinc Oxide Mineral Oil	Ointment
Anusol		Phenylephrine**	Suppository
Fleet Medicated Wipes		Witch Hazel Glycerin	Pads
Hemorid for Women		Pramoxine* Phenylephrine** Zinc Oxide Petrolatum	Cream
Hemorid for Women		Phenylephrine** Zinc Oxide	Suppository
Lanacane		Benzocaine	Cream
Nupercainal		Dibucaine*** Lanolin Petrolatum Mineral Oil	Ointment
Nupercainal		Zinc Oxide Cocoa Butter	Suppository

continued

TABLE 9-1: Common Hemorrhoidal Products (continued)

National Brand Products	Eckerd Brand Products	Ingredient(s)	Dosage Form(s)
Preparation H		Glycerin Petrolatum Lanolin	Cream
Preparation H	Hemorrhoidal Ointment	Mineral Oil Petrolatum Lanolin, Glycerin	Ointment
Preparation H	Hemorrhoidal Suppository	Cocoa Butter	Suppository
Tucks		Witch Hazel Glycerin	Pads, Gel
Vaseline Pure	Petroleum Jelly	Petrolatum	Ointment

*Products that contain pramoxine and benzocaine have been known to cause allergic reactions and may actually cause irritation, burning, or itching. If this occurs, discontinue use.

**Products that contain phenyleprhine or ephedrine should not be used by persons who have diabetes, high blood pressure, heart disease, or hyperthyroidism as possible side effects may occur.

***Products that contain dibucaine are extremely toxic to young children. Seizures, cardiac arrest, and death have resulted just minutes after ingesting small amounts of this ingredient. This product must now be sold in child-proof packaging. Keep this and all medications out of the reach of children.

TABLE 9-2: Bulk-Forming Laxatives to Ease Symptoms

National Brand Products	Eckerd Brand Products	Dosage Form(s)
Citrucel (Regular and Sugar Free)		Powder
Equalactin		Chewable Tablet
Fibercon	Fiber Tablets	Tablet
Fiberall		Tablet
Fiberall (Oatmeal Raisin)		Wafer
Fiberall (Orange)		Powder
Konsyl		Powder
Konsyl Fiber		Tablet
Metamucil Fiber (Apple Crisp)		Wafer
Metamucil (Original, Sugar Free)	Natural Fiber Powder	Packet
Metamucil (Original Texture)	Natural Fiber (Citrus)	Powder
Metamucil (Smooth Texture-Orange, Regular)	Smooth Natural Fiber Powder	Powder
Metamucil (Smooth Texture-Sugar Free, Citrus)	Smooth Natural Fiber Powder, Sugar Free	Packet
Perdiem		Granule
Perdiem Fiber		Granule

Notes Pertaining to Your Personal OTC Drug Preferences

_____

_____

_____

_____

_____

_____

_____

_____

_____

_____

_____

_____

_____

_____

_____

_____

_____

_____

_____

_____

_____

_____

_____

_____

It's right at Eckerd!

www.eckerd.com

We are continually updating the information in this book and we invite you to stay up-to-date on information pertaining to over-the-counter medications and products when you visit us at our **Home Page** on the **World Wide Web**.

At the Eckerd Home Page, you can find all of the information in this book, plus current information on the new over-the-counter medications and products that are coming to our stores every day.

You can find the location of every Eckerd pharmacy. In addition, you can find features of special interest—health facts, a list of healthcare links, and you can access the Rx Advisor database. You can also refill prescriptions on-line and learn more about living with diabetes.

Why not set a bookmark at **www.eckerd.com**—and visit us often.

ECKERD
It's right at Eckerd!

Chapter Ten

Choosing Vitamin, Mineral, and Herb Supplements

Vitamins and **minerals** are required by the body and are responsible for helping to maintain health.

Studies have shown that nutrients from whole foods are better absorbed and utilized by the body than are the nutrients obtained from supplements. One problem, however, is that vitamins and minerals may be depleted from some foods when they are cooked or processed. Even the best eaters may not be getting enough nutrition from their food. Therefore, some individuals may need to supplement their diet with vitamins and minerals.

A **balanced diet,** as defined by the U.S. government, is a diet that contains 100% of the **recommended daily allowance** (RDA) based on a diet of 2,000 calories for women and 3,000 calories for men. The RDAs were developed to serve as nutritional guidelines and to help prevent vitamin and mineral deficiencies. They are based on the needs of an average healthy person. The RDAs do not take stress levels or disease into consideration or the fact, that many Americans smoke or consume alcohol. All of these factors may affect the amount of nutrients required for each individual.

Who Should Take Vitamin and Mineral Supplements?

Although vitamins and minerals are safe and effective for most individuals, there are specific groups of people who benefit most from supplementation. These groups include the following:

- People who do not eat a properly "balanced diet" (shown in Chart 10-1)
- Children
- Women who are pregnant or nursing
- Women of childbearing age
- Postmenopausal women

10

◀ Elderly persons
◀ Smokers
◀ People who consume an excessive amount of alcohol

The chart below represents the four main food groups and the number of servings per day needed for a well-balanced diet.

CHART 10-1: The Well-Balanced Diet

Food Group	Number Services/Day
Fruits/Vegetables	5
Dairy	2–3 *
Meat/Protein	2–3
Whole Grains	6–11

* More dairy products are needed for children or for women who are pregnant or nursing.

Many supplements are currently available, and choosing the best one can be difficult. The key to choosing the best vitamin or mineral supplement is to choose one that contains the appropriate amount of ingredient(s).

Most vitamins will contain between 100% to 300% of the RDA. A supplement should contain at least 100% of the RDA for each ingredient. Some ingredients contain up to 300% of the RDA, which is safe for most nutrients. The label on vitamin or mineral supplements will show the RDA for each ingredient, the amount of each ingredient contained in that product, and the percent of RDA for each ingredient.

Any supplement that contains more than 300% of the RDA for any nutrient, except the anti-oxidants, for example, should not be taken. One reason not to take high doses of vitamins is that an excess of one vitamin may decrease the absorption or cause malabsorption of another vitamin. Also, excessive amounts of some vitamins such as A, D, E, and K may cause side effects.

Types of Vitamins

Vitamins are classified as fat-soluble or water-soluble. **Fat-soluble** vitamins include A, D, E, and K. All other vitamins are **water-soluble**. Fat-soluble vitamins can be stored in the fat reserves of the body. An overdose may lead to problems.

Water-soluble vitamins are absorbed by the body, if and as the body needs them. The excess amount of water-soluble vitamins not used by the body is excreted through the urine.

Dosing and Side Effects of Vitamin and Mineral Supplements

Many nutritional supplements may cause stomach upset. This may be eliminated by taking the supplement after eating (unless instructed otherwise), or by taking the supplement in divided doses over the course of the day. Supplements should not be taken with tea or coffee because these drinks can interfere with the absorption of the supplements.

It is important for you to know that some nutritional supplements may cause the urine to become yellowish-brown and have a strong odor. This is normal and may continue as long as you take the vitamins or minerals.

Vitamins are not recommended for everyone. Some vitamins interact with medications or certain disease states. Consult your Eckerd Pharmacist or physician before taking any nutritional supplement.

Medical Benefits and Other Claims of Supplements

There are many claims that appear on various vitamin and mineral bottles that have been scientifically found to be not true. For example, many products claim to be **stress formulated,** but no product has ever been proven to truly ease stress. Some products are often referred to as **natural** or **organic.** These products are often much more expensive and are no more effective than synthetics.

The body cannot tell the difference between a natural-source vitamin or mineral and a synthetic-source vitamin or mineral. Do not fall prey to these types of advertising ploys. A plain tablet of vitamin C is as good as any "hyped-up" version.

Vitamins and Minerals in the News

The topic of vitamins has become a real issue in today's news. Many manufacturers make so many claims and references about their products that it can become really confusing. Although studies have shown support toward improved health due to the use of some vitamins, further research is needed.

The following section outlines some of the most advertised vitamins and minerals and their claims.

Antioxidants—Antioxidant vitamins include vitamins A, E, and C. Antioxidants are believed to protect the body from substances known as **free radicals.** Free radicals may increase the risk of heart disease, diabetes, and cancer. More evidence is needed to show whether antioxidants decrease the risk of these diseases.

Dehydroepiandrosterone (DHEA)—DHEA has been advertised as a **weight-loss aid** and as having beneficial effects on aging and disease. However, these uses have not been proven. There are many side effects associated with the use of DHEA. Side effects of DHEA in women include acne, hair loss, hirsutism (growth of unwanted hair), and the deepening of the voice. In both men and women, DHEA could stimulate the growth of some cancers.

Folic acid—Folic acid has been shown to help decrease the risk of birth defects. Because of this finding, increased amounts of folic acid is recommended during pregnancy. Women who are pregnant or are planning to become pregnant should consult their physician to determine how much folic acid is needed.

Chromium—Chromium has been promoted for lowering cholesterol, producing weight loss, and increasing muscle mass, but these claims have not been proven. Diabetics should not take chromium without consulting with their physician.

Selenium—Research investigating selenium's effect on cancer suggests that selenium may have the potential to prevent cancer. Selenium is thought to have antioxidant properties like that of vitamins A, E, and C. A recent study found that individuals who were taking selenium had a lower incidence of certain types of cancer than individuals who were not taking selenium. However, other studies showed no benefit. Research is needed to determine whether selenium actually prevents cancer and, if so, which types of cancer selenium may be effective against. Beware! High doses of selenium can cause weak fingernails, hair loss, garlic breath, and fatigue.

Zinc—Zinc is believed to increase the body's immune system, promote wound healing, and aid in skin conditions. One of the most publicized uses of zinc has been the claim that zinc decreases the duration of the common cold. However, it is not known whether this is true. Zinc taken in high doses can cause anemia, mood alteration, and increased cholesterol. Individuals should check with their physician before taking zinc supplements.

Single-Source and Multi-Source Vitamins and Minerals

Many products are available as single-source supplements. For example, your physician may recommend that you take a calcium supplement. Conveniently, you are able to purchase a bottle of calcium. However, if your physician recommends you take several vitamins or minerals, your best bet may be to buy a multi-source supplement, a product that contains several different vitamins and minerals. This will be cheaper than buying several products in an effort to obtain all of the ingredients you need and you will only need to take one tablet instead of taking two or more tablets.

A good multi-source supplement should contain the following vitamins and minerals: **A, B_1, B_2, B_6, B_{12}, C, D, E, niacin, biotin, calcium, chromium, copper, folic acid, iodine, iron, magnesium, manganese, molybdenum, pantothenic acid, selenium,** and **zinc** in the proper amounts.

Again, look at the label and make sure that there is at least 100% of the RDA for each ingredient. Many products may contain small amounts of other ingredients that may not be necessary for your needs and may increase the cost. Therefore, you should compare products to determine which best suits your needs. Other ingredients, such as sugar or starch, may be present. These ingredients are present in such small amounts that they will have no effect on the user.

Tables 10-1 (page 138) and 10-2 (page 139) list single-source vitamins and minerals, their food source, the RDA, and their indication(s) for use. The information in these tables is based on the nutritional requirements for an average adult.

Summary

When taken properly, vitamins and minerals can be safe and effective. They should not be taken in high doses in an effort to self-treat an illness or disease without first consulting with your Eckerd Pharmacist or physician. Most importantly, vitamin and mineral supplements should not be taken to replace proper nutrition.

The key to staying healthy is eating well and exercising. A well-balanced diet will provide the body with the proper amounts of vitamins and minerals.

Herbal Medicine

For thousands of years, plants have been used in the treatment of a variety of disorders. Many of the medications used today were derived from plants. For example, aspirin was made from the dried bark of white willow trees.

Currently, there is increased interest in taking herbs to prevent and treat illness. Medicinal herbs are botanicals used to treat some illnesses and to attain or maintain a condition of improved health. There is a great deal of controversy as to whether herbal remedies are beneficial. This controversy exists because the effectiveness and safety of herbs has not been proven.

While most herbs are generally safe, some may cause severe problems. Before taking herbs, people need to understand how they should be taken. For instance, people need to know what dose of herbal medication they should take, the side effects of herbs, and which medications and diseases or illnesses interact with herbs. The following is a list of guidelines for using medicinal herbs.

- ◀ Do not exceed the recommended dose.
- ◀ Stop taking the herb immediately if side effects occur.
- ◀ If you are taking other medications, talk to your pharmacist or physician before taking herbs.
- ◀ Herbs should be purchased from reliable sources. There are many differences in strength, quality, and purity of herbal products. Before taking an herbal product, ask the pharmacist if the manufacturer of that product is a reliable and trusted source.
- ◀ Make sure the herbal product you buy is a standardized product. If a product is standardized, it means that each capsule or tablet contains a specific quantity of active ingredients. If a product is not standardized, the quality and effects of the product may be questionable.
- ◀ Herbs should not be used during pregnancy or nursing.
- ◀ Herbs should not be used by infants or young children.
- ◀ Herbs used to treat serious health problems should be used only on the advice and supervision of a physician.
- ◀ Herbs that do not have an expiration date printed on the label should be thrown out if more than one year old.
- ◀ Herbal products, as with all medication products should be stored in a cool, dry place and out of the reach of children.

Table 10-3 (page 140) lists herbs that are considered **safe**, their uses, and precautions.

Table 10-4 (page 141) lists herbs which are considered **unsafe**, their "so-called" uses, and their side effects.

Summary

Some herbs may be effective in relieving certain illnesses. However, some herbs are not safe or effective. Before taking an herbal remedy, you should discuss with your Eckerd Pharmacist or physician whether a particular herb is safe, effective, and if it could interact with any disease you may have or any medications you are taking.

Before purchasing an herbal product, be certain that it is produced by a reliable and trusted manufacturer and that is a standardized product. Remember, herbs are not miraculous cure-alls. Herbs may help some health problems, but they should not be used to treat serious illnesses without the advice of a physician.

TABLE 10-1: Single-Source Vitamins

Vitamins	Source	RDA	Indication for Use
A (Beta-carotene)	Fish, dairy products, organ meats, dark leafy vegetables, squash, carrots, pumpkins	5,000 IU	Proper eye growth, prevent dry eyes or night blindness, and poor bone/tooth development
B1 (Thiamine)	Pork, beef, beans, peas, and hulls of rice grains	1.5 mg	Prevent beriberi, heart problems, nausea, fatigue, weight loss
B2 (Riboflavin)	Meats, poultry, fish, dairy products, grains, cereals, green vegetables	1.7 mg	Prevents cracks and sores at corners of the mouth and dermatitis
B3 (Niacin, nicotinic acid)	Meats, fish, cereals, grains, green vegetables, legumes	19 mg	Prevents pellagra, dermatitis, mental problems, diarrhea, anemia
B6 (Pyridoxine)	Meats, nuts, lentils, bananas, avocados, potatoes, cereals	2 mg	Prevents anemia and malabsorption
B12 (Cyanocobalamin)	Meats, oysters, clams	2 mg	Prevents anemia, dermatitis, nerve damage, fatigue
Biotin	Liver, egg yolk, yeast, salmon, soy, carrots, bananas	100–200 mg	Prevents hair loss, dermatitis, anorexia
C (Ascorbic acid)	Citrus fruits, strawberries, red and yellow peppers, spinach, broccoli	60 mg	Prevents scurvy, skin problems, anemia; promotes wound healing
D (Calciferol)	Milk, dairy products	200–400 IU	Prevents rickets, osteomalacia, osteoporosis
E (d-alpha-tocopherol)	Margarines (plant oils), nuts, vegetable oils, green vegetables, grains, wheat germ	15 IU	Prevents anemia, muscle weakness
Folic acid (Folate, folacin)	Liver, leafy vegetables, beef, veal, legumes, eggs, whole-grain, cereals, yeast, some fruits	200 mg	Prevents anemia, nerve damage, mood disorders, malabsorption, weakness, birth disorders
Pantothenic acid (Calcium pantothenate)	Meat, eggs, liver, legumes, cereal, grains, vegetables, milk	4–7 mg	Prevents anemia

TABLE 10-2: Single-Source Minerals

Minerals	Source	RDA	Indication for Use
Calcium	Milk, dairy products	800–1200 mg	Prevents osteoporosis, weak bones and teeth
Chromium (GTF, nicotinate, picolinate, chromic chloride)	Fish, grains, liver, milk	50–200 mg	Prevents diabetes, poor glucose tolerance, heart disease
Copper	Organ meats, shellfish, nuts, legumes, chocolate	1.5–3 mg	Prevents central nervous system lesions, aneurysms, anemia
Iodine	Iodized salt	150 mg	Prevents goiter, cretinism
Iron (Ferrous fumarate, gluconate, sulfate)	Meats, vegetables (spinach)	10 mg (men) 15 mg (women) 30 mg (pregnancy)	Prevents anemia, fatigue
Magnesium (citrate, oxide, hydroxide)	Vegetables, nuts, legumes	350 mg (men) 280 mg (women)	Prevents arrhythmias, hair loss, muscle weakness, spasms, confusion, GI problems
Manganese (gluconate)	Vegetables, fruits, legumes, nuts, cereals	2–5 mg	Prevents growth, retardation, birth defects
Molybdenum	Milk, organ meats, breads, cereals, beans	75–250 mg	Prevents stunted growth
Selenium	Meats, seafood, cereals	70 mg (men) 50–55 mg (women)	Prevents liver and muscle damage, cardiomyopathy
Zinc (gluconate, picolinate)	Liver, meats, oysters, legumes, nuts	15 mg	Prevents anemia, stunted growth, decrease in sense of taste; promotes wound healing

TABLE 10-3: Medicinal Herbs Considered Safe

Name	Uses	Precautions
Chamomile	Aids digestion, calms an upset stomach; used topically it promotes healing and decreases inflammation	May cause reactions in people allergic to plants in the daisy family
Echinacea	Stimulates the immune system; helpful for treating colds and flu	May cause reactions in people allergic to plants in the sunflower family
Feverfew	Helps prevent and reduce symptoms of migraines	Some products do not contain enough of the active ingredient to get the desired effect; leaves should not contain less than 0.2% parthenolide
Garlic	Lowers blood cholesterol and helps prevent blood clots	None
Ginger	Reduces symptoms of nausea and motion sickness	None
Ginko biloba	Improves circulation; increases blood flow to the brain; may help conditions such as varicose veins, dizziness, and short-term memory loss	Should be standardized to 24%
Milk thistle	Protects the liver against damage by toxins; may help in treatment of hepatitis and cirrhosis	Do not take without talking to your physician
Saw palmetto	Treatment for benign prostatic hypertrophy	Should be standardized to contain 85%—95% of fatty acids and sterols
Valerian	Mild tranquilizer and sleep aid	None
Ginseng	Aids in resistance to various kinds of stress	An excess amount over a period of time may cause high blood pressure and nervousness; should be standardized to contain 7% ginsenosides
Peppermint	Aids digestion, soothes gastrointestinal upset	Excessive use may cause heartburn

TABLE 10-4: Medicinal Herbs Considered Unsafe

Name	So-Called Uses	Side Effects
Borage	Diuretic, anti-diarrheal	Safety and efficacy has not been determined; contains toxic ingredients
Calamus	Digestive aid; treatment for fever	May cause cancer
Chaparral	Anti-cancer	Not proven effective; may cause liver damage
Coltsfoot	Relieve cough and bronchial congestion	Not proven safe; may cause liver damage
Comfrey	Wound healing	Not proven safe; may cause liver damage
Germander	Weight-loss aid	Not proven safe or effective; may cause liver damage
Licorice	Expectorant, ulcer treatment	Prolonged use can lead to serious electrolyte imbalances
Life root	Treatment for menstrual irregularity	Not proven safe or effective; may cause liver damage
Ma huang (ephedra)	Bronchodilator; boost energy and performance; aid in weight loss; improve athletic performance	Contains a stimulant that can raise blood pressure and cause palpitations, nerve damage, muscle injury, stroke, or psychotic episodes if taken in excess; unsafe for those suffering from high blood pressure, diabetes, or thyroid disease; should not be taken with caffeine
Pokeweed	Anti-cancer; treatment for rheumatoid arthritis	Not safe or effective; fatal poisoning
Sassafras	Stimulant; antispasmodic; treatment for rheumatoid arthritis	Not safe or effective; may cause cancer

Index

EMERGENCY NUMBERS

9-1-1

Ambulance _____

Fire _____

Police _____

Poison

Poison Center: _____

Doctor

Doctor: _____

Phone: _____

Pediatrician: _____

Phone: _____

ECKERD
It's right at Eckerd!

My Closest Eckerd Pharmacy:

Address: _____

Phone: _____

Notes Pertaining to Your Personal OTC Drug Preferences

_____

_____

_____

_____

_____

_____

_____

_____

_____

_____

_____

_____

_____

_____

_____

_____

_____

Notes Pertaining to Your Personal OTC Drug Preferences

_____

_____

_____

_____

_____

_____

_____

_____

_____

_____

_____

_____

_____

_____

_____

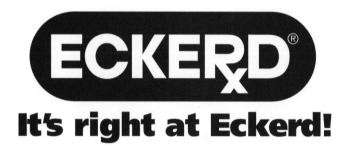

CONFUSED? About Nutrition

Fats, Oils, & Sweets
USE SPARINGLY

KEY
▲ Fat (naturally occurring and added)   □ Sugars (added)
These symbols show fat & added sugars in foods.

Milk, Yogurt, & Cheese Group
2-3 SERVINGS

Meat, Poultry, Fish, Dry Beans, Eggs, & Nuts Group
2-3 SERVINGS

Vegetable Group
3-5 SERVINGS

Fruit Group
2-4 SERVINGS

Bread, Cereal, Rice, & Pasta Group
6-11 SERVINGS

Source: U.S. Department of Agriculture/U.S. Department of Health and Human Services

Good nutrition is a key to good health, but today's on-the-go lifestyle makes it difficult to maintain a well-balanced diet. Good health should not be taken for granted. The Food Guide Pyramid, developed by the U.S. Department of Agriculture and the U.S. Department of Health and Human Services, can help you choose a healthful diet that fits your lifestyle.

VITAMINS

Believe it or not, only 10% of Americans eat the recommended daily requirement of 5 to 9 servings of fruits and vegetables. That's probably why 69% of Americans complement their diet with nutritional supplements. Some of today's health-conscious people choose Theragran®, the high potency multivitamin with more B_1, B_2 and C than other leading brands.

VITAMIN/MINERAL TIPS

- Choose a supplement that's complete, providing at least 20 vitamins and minerals that help maintain good health.
- Select a supplement that contains the antioxidant nutrients beta carotene and vitamins C and E. The label may state the percent of vitamin A from beta carotene. That's because the body converts beta carotene to vitamin A.
- Be sure the expiration date on the supplement has not been reached. Supplements lose their potency over time.
- Choose a supplement that's easy to swallow.
- Avoid supplements that contain substances with no proven benefits (e.g., PABA and lecithin).
- There is no nutritional advantage to choosing a "natural" vitamin over a synthetic one. And it isn't necessary to choose a supplement because it is free of sugar or starch. Small amounts of sugar and starch are sometimes added so the nutrients in a supplement are better absorbed.

Theragran's Guide To Good Nutrition

VITAMIN/MINERAL	DIETARY SOURCE	FUNCTIONS
Beta Carotene	Carrots, sweet potatoes, spinach, other dark green leafy and yellow/orange vegetables, cantaloupe, mango, apricots, papaya	An antioxidant protecting cells and organs from free radical damage. Converted as needed into vitamin A in the body.
C	Citrus fruits, melons, berries, potatoes, kiwi fruit, cabbage, broccoli, tomatoes, fruit juices, fortified cereals	Involved in forming and maintaining collagen, a protein that helps support body cells. Needed to repair bones and teeth and to heal cuts and bruises. Helps iron absorption. As an antioxidant, assists in protecting cells and organs from damage.
E	Vegetable oils, nuts, wheat germ, whole grains, green leafy vegetables	Needed for healthy blood cells and tissues. Acts as an antioxidant to protect cells in essential fatty acids from damaging free radicals.
Folic Acid (Folate)	Leafy green vegetables, oranges, liver, dried beans and peas	Helps form DNA and RNA. Part of the formation and breakdown of amino acids in protein. Necessary for manufacturing red blood cells. Protects against certain birth defects, namely spinal bifida.
Calcium	Milk and dairy products, canned sardines and salmon with bones, tofu (soybean curd) made with calcium	Strengthens bones and teeth. Needed for blood clotting, muscle contractions, normal heart beat, proper nerve function. Helps regulate blood pressure.
Iron	Liver, kidney, beef, dried peas and beans, enriched cereals, green leafy vegetables	An essential component of hemoglobin, which carries oxygen to all body cells and organs.
B_1 (Thiamin)	Whole grains, dried beans and peas, pork organ meats, enriched grain products	Works with other B vitamins to convert carbohydrates from food into energy. Needed by the brain, nervous system, and muscles.
B_3 (Niacin)	Meats, fish, liver, dried beans and peas fortified grain products	Needed for healthy skin, nervous system, and digestive tract. Active in metabolism of carbohydrates, fats and proteins.

Recent Arthritis Treatment Guidelines Recommend Tylenol First Instead of Aspirin.

Is the pain of osteoarthritis getting in the way of your life? Then it's time to talk to your doctor about a pain reliever that can help.

The American College of Rheumatology* —the leading organization of arthritis doctors—recently published guidelines on osteoarthritis treatment. And their first choice for pain relief isn't aspirin... *it's the medicine in Tylenol.†*

Osteoarthritis: The Real Problem Is Pain.

Doctors once believed osteoarthritis was an inflammatory condition like the more serious rheumatoid arthritis. That's why they often treated osteoarthritis with anti-inflammatory drugs.

Today, doctors have new insights into what causes the pain of osteoarthritis. Specifically, it's *not inflammation* that generally causes this pain. Rather, it's the wearing away of the protective cartilage tissue inside the joints.

Tylenol: First Choice for the Pain.

Since osteoarthritis is primarily a problem of pain and not inflammation, the American College of Rheumatology guidelines specify that pain relief be the primary goal of drug therapy. And the first choice for pain relief is the medicine in Tylenol.

Tylenol provides effective relief of the nagging, aching pain of osteoarthritis. And, because Tylenol works differently than anti-inflammatory drugs, it won't cause stomach irritation the way aspirin sometimes can.

Talk to Your Doctor.

In addition to choosing the right pain reliever, controlling your weight and exercising are both important parts of the American College of Rheumatology treatment guidelines. So talk to your doctor about getting started in these two areas. And remember: doctors recommend Tylenol more than any other pain reliever.

*The American College of Rheumatology is an independent professional, medical, and scientific society which does not guarantee, warrant, or endorse any commercial product or service.

The Pain Reliever Hospitals Use Most.

TYLENOL®

pain reliever

†Use only as directed. © McN-PPC, Inc. 1997

MAKE MAALOX® THE FAST CHOICE FOR YOU.

Maalox® Health Tip

Many people regularly experience heartburn. One typical cause is when acid from the stomach backs up into the swallowing tube, called the esophagus. Things to try on your own:

Leading The Way To Relief

- Take an acid relief product
- Monitor the medications you are taking - some may irriatate the lining of the stomach or esophagus
- Watch your fat intake and consumption of alcohol
- Don't lay down or go to bed right after a meal
- Quit smoking

Maalox® Antacid

GREAT NEW FLAVOR!

Refreshing Lemon

FAST RELIEF of Heartburn and Acid Indigestion!

ONE MINUTE **Maalox®™**

Use only as directed.

Take it at night and have a good morning.

Vicks® NyQuil® relieves your sniffling, sneezing, coughing, aching, stuffy head and fever... at night. Which means you can get the sleep you need to turn the next morning into a good morning.

NyQuil and DayQuil®. Nighttime, daytime, all the time cold relief.

People Today Are Living Longer and Healthier Lives.

At *Nature Made*, We Like To Think We've Been A Part Of It.

Nature Made vitamin and mineral supplements are recommended by pharmacists more than 1,000 times a day. And as America's best-selling broadline supplement brand, Nature Made offers more than 100 different vitamins, minerals and essential nutrients to helps you achieve your nutritional and lifestyle goals.

Children's Advil®. The first choice of physicians in an important study.

In a major study, Children's Advil was the fever medicine doctors preferred 2 to 1 over Children's Tylenol® for treating sick children.*

Controls fevers faster.

In a recent study, Children's Advil controlled fevers almost 45 minutes faster than Children's Tylenol.† So children can start feeling better sooner. Which is something parents will really appreciate.

45 minutes faster

Controls fevers longer.

And Children's Advil has the advantage of 8-hour dosing. That's up to twice as long as Children's Tylenol.

1 DOSE		
Children's Advil		8 hrs
Children's Tylenol	4 hrs	

Safe on a child's stomach.

The fact is, Children's Advil is as safe on a child's stomach as Children's Tylenol.

Faster, longer fever relief that's safe on a child's stomach adds up to one thing…better. Exactly what we want for our children.

Children's **Advil**
Fever Reducer
Pain Reliever
Lasts up to 8 Hours

Children's Advil®.
Just a better fever medicine.™

Take Good Care of Yourself and Your Family with Sunbeam

Save $5 on any one of these
Health at Home by Sunbeam products.

Ultrasonic Humidifier	Soft Touch Heating Pad	Blood Pressure Monitor
Model# 694	Model# 790	Model# 7652/7654

VITAMINS

Your Health. Your Life.®

Today's lifestyles demand the most from your time, your energy and your body. To help maintain your health and vitality, a healthy diet, exercise and Your Life® vitamins and supplements belong in your daily routine.

From the superior formulations of our complete line of vitamins, to symptom specific herbs and supplements, our advanced science makes Your Life® nothing but the best.

1-800-533-VITA
Monday thru Friday, 8 am to 5 pm EST

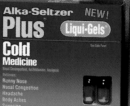

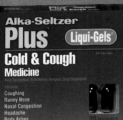

Get Fast Relief

Get Alka-Seltzer Plus®

SLEEP LIKE YOU'VE NEVER HAD HEARTBURN.

Now you can sleep the whole night without waking with heartburn. All it takes is one tiny Pepcid AC tablet. That's because Pepcid AC can prevent heartburn all night long. Something antacids can't claim.

So when you know you're having a dinner that might cause heartburn, just take a Pepcid AC an hour before you eat. That way you get to sleep without waking in the middle of the night with heartburn. And Pepcid AC has no drug interaction warnings, so it can be taken with many frequently prescribed medications.

Pepcid AC will have you eating like your old self, sleeping like you never even <u>had</u> heartburn.

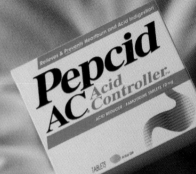

You can be heartburn free with Pepcid AC.

If dairy food is one big problem, take one little caplet.

If dairy foods do a number on your stomach (you know—gas, bloating, diarrhea), you may be lactose intolerant. It's a common problem. But here's a solution. Lactaid® Ultra.

Just one little caplet lets you digest dairy foods easily and naturally. We're talking about all the delicious dairy foods you crave. Ice cream, milk, pizza. So dig into dairy. With Lactaid Ultra. Go on, enjoy dairy again.

For a free sample call toll free,

1-888-ULTRA-NOW

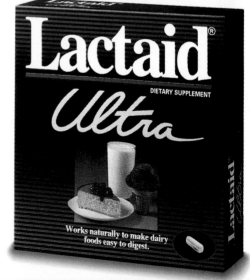

SAVE $10 ON YOUR FLU SHOT WHEN YOU PURCHASE ANY 2 AFRIN® PRODUCTS (except trial sizes)

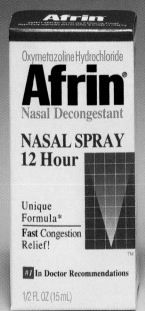
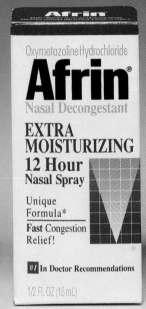
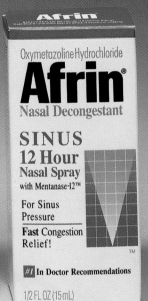

Afrin® Nasal Spray - Number One in Doctor and Pharmacist recommendations.

Afrin® relieves your nasal congestion due to colds & flu within 5 minutes, without drowsiness. That's four times faster than the leading cold tablet. Receive a $10 rebate check for your flu shot, when you purchase any two (2) AFRIN® products at *ECKERD* (except trial sizes).

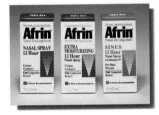